HOME-SEWN
French Style

HOME-SEWN
French Style

35 STEP-BY-STEP BEAUTIFUL & CHIC SEWING PROJECTS
INCLUDES 6 FULL-SIZE PATTERNS

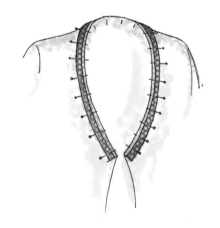

AMELIE MORIN-FONTAINE

CICO BOOKS
LONDON NEW YORK

For N and K

Published in 2014 by CICO Books
An imprint of Ryland Peters & Small
519 Broadway, 5th Floor, New York NY 10012
20–21 Jockey's Fields, London WC1R 4BW
www.rylandpeters.com

10 9 8 7 6 5 4 3 2 1

A CIP catalog record for this book is available from the Library of Congress and the British Library.

ISBN: 978-1-78249-083-8

Printed in China

Editor: Sarah Hoggett
Designer: Tom Forge
Step illustration: Harriet de Winton
Pattern illustration: Stephen Dew
Additional illustration: Michael Hill
Photographer: Caroline Arber
Stylists: Nel Haynes and Catherine Woram

about the author

Amélie Morin-Fontaine started sewing over 10 years ago and has never stopped since. She has written a blog on sewing since 2008 (mydaruma.wordpress.com). Having worked as a library curator for 12 years, she has now co-founded an e-book project in France, www.citronours.fr, and her e-book *Bien débuter en couture* ("Sewing for Beginners") was released in August 2013. Born in France, she lived in the US and Canada as a child, and in the UK during her studies, but she has now returned to France, where she lives with her husband and daughter.

contents

introduction

French style can be a little unsettling and paradoxical. It is both smart and relaxed. It is about effortless elegance and is usually defined as chic... but never at the expense of comfort. In its countryside version, it's a mix of the rustic and the refined. In a nutshell, it's a fragile equilibrium based on the French *art de vivre*. I believe that is what makes it so appealing worldwide and why it is such a great source of inspiration for the home.

I was born and raised in France, where I still live today, but as a child and young adult I lived abroad for several years. This expatriate experience helped me understand French culture better: stepping away from what I had always known—and had probably taken for granted—was a great opportunity to fully comprehend and appreciate the specifics of French style. Sewing being a great way to interpret and experiment, I am now very happy to share my insider's view of French style and hope you will be inspired to recreate it yourself.

An introductory styling section will give you the basics of French style. To help you recreate this style right away, I have put together 35 projects for your home and wardrobe. Each one is beautifully photographed and comes with detailed step-by-step instructions plus charming and informative illustrations that will guide you through the sewing process.

The projects are organized in five chapters, each summing up one aspect of French style: *Les châteaux de la Loire, A la campagne, La belle Provence, Au bord de la mer*, and *Paris, je t'aime*. An approximate level of skill and sewing time are suggested to help you select your next project. At the back of the book, beginners will find an illustrated section with basic sewing guidelines. This section also includes some more advanced techniques used in several of the projects.

Following the guidelines and steps in this book, I am sure you will make beautiful home-sewn French-style projects—and, I hope, be inspired to devise your own.

creating French style

If you were to visit Normandy, Paris, Provence, or the French Riviera, chances are you would detect very distinct styles of architecture, furniture, and decoration. However, some common features stand out. Let me guide you through the basics of French style.

Use natural materials and vintage accessories

Natural materials set the overall mood of the French home. That is especially true in the countryside. The construction of the French house itself usually sets the tone. A beamed ceiling, a stone fireplace, and a wooden staircase are a good start. Natural stone floors and terracotta tiles are common in the entranceway and kitchen, while solid oak planks give warmth and comfort to the bedrooms.

Of course, time-worn accessories and vintage furniture are of the utmost importance. To scatter them in different rooms of the house is an easy way to recreate the French *art de vivre*. Woven baskets, copper pots, antique plates hanging from walls, rush-woven chair seats, solid oak kitchen tables, rustic wood burning stoves: all speak of the French countryside.

Parisian style can easily be recreated using the right accessories: add a French urban touch to your home with café tables and bistro coat hangers, large vintage clocks, delicate light fixtures, large *ardoise* blackboards, and vintage advertisement posters.

This craving for authentic natural materials and vintage objects also applies to fabrics in the home. Pure cottons and linens are praised in every room. It's great if you can get your hands on some antique fabric, but most of the time that will not be an option. Don't worry and simply favor the quality of the fabric over any ostentatious print. Keep the lines clean and soft, but use the best-quality fabric or most natural fibers you can find.

Learn to navigate colors and prints

As with materials, natural and subdued colors are great options. Cream, ecru, beige, and off-white are commonplace in the French home and are often mixed together with interesting results.

If you are to redecorate a room, play with a full range of textures rather than mixing too many colors. In that regard, the rich aristocratic style of the Loire valley is particularly relevant: velvet, brocade, and lustrous silk can all be mixed together, as long as it is done in a monochromatic color scheme to preserve elegance.

Provençal style itself offers a color palette inspired by nature: vivid orange, olive green, bright yellow, sky blue, and soft lavender. It is as if these bold colors bring the olive groves, lavender fields, and mimosa flowers of the area right into your home!

On the other side of the color spectrum, deep red appeals to the French sense of romance and adventure. Don't hesitate to use this bold color, whether in solid or printed fabrics, to recreate the glamorous atmosphere of Paris.

There is a wide range of prints to choose from. Whatever you select, let prints be the star of your projects, and shy away from the tendency to mix too many together. Using them wisely also has a lot to do with context. Checks are mostly found in the kitchen: hand towels, tablecloths, or any food-related accessory look great in red checks. Traditional Provençal prints provide us with delicate floral designs, often embellished by vertical lines, and are especially nice in the living room or in the garden.

Of course, some traditional prints are particularly famous and now part of the French heritage—notably toile, ticking, and Breton stripes.

Toile de Jouy is a richly decorated fabric that was first manufactured at the end of the 18th century in the town of Jouy-en-Josas, not far from the royal palace of Versailles. Usually portraying pastoral scenes in monochrome colors on a white or ecru backround, toile de Jouy is typical of the Loire valley style. It will definitely give a traditional and aristocratic French feel to any living room. Remember that there's no need to have antique furniture to match this fabric or to go for frills or gathers: it's actually very interesting to give the detailed pattern of toile de Jouy your full attention and to select sober projects. Toile de Jouy is used for all sorts of decoration, mostly curtains, chairs pads, and cushions, lampshades and tapestry. Lastly, note that it is very difficult to mix different toiles together. Stay within one color range for optimum results.

French ticking, known in French as *toile à matelas* ("mattress toile"), is a traditional heavyweight fabric that was originally used to make mattresses. The authentic stripes are white and gray and printed in a specific sequence. There are other kinds of vintage ticking with red colors and floral prints. They are becoming rare but can still be found in antique shops and, on lucky days, in garage sales. All ticking fabrics are very resistant and ideal for adding a sober French touch to a room. Note that the graphic stripes look best on large projects.

Breton stripes have truly become part of French cultural heritage. They were originally introduced in the late nineteenth century on sailors' tops in Brittany. The working mariner's top (*la marinière*) was then popularized over the years with the help of Coco Chanel and Jean-Paul Gaultier, who transformed the way we looked at it for ever. For a chic French coastal look, you can't go wrong with Breton stripes!

Last but not least, remember that French style comes down to effortless chic. Well-selected colors, natural materials and fibers, vintage accessories, and traditional prints will help greatly. But French style is also about restraint and confidence. The best way to achieve this stylish equilibrium is to experiment...

So let's start sewing!

les châteaux de la Loire

Amboise, Chambord, Chenonceau, Villandry. . . The Loire valley castles are all about the refinement of the Renaissance. How about adapting this elegant style to contemporary life?

cushion cover

There's no need to have antique furniture to match this richly decorated fabric. It's actually very interesting to give the detailed pattern of toile de Jouy your full attention and to use it for sober projects, like this square chair-pad cover. Because of its light background color, it's important to be able to wash projects made with toile de Jouy. Using a zipper as the closure makes it easy to remove the cover; furthermore, it is the most effective way of dealing with thick cushion pads.

You will need

Two 17 x 1¾-in. (43 x 4.5-cm) strips of fabric

Two 17 x 2½-in. (43 x 6-cm) strips of fabric

One 17 x 34½-in. (43 x 86-cm) rectangle of fabric

One 12-in. (30-cm) closed-end zipper

Foam pad measuring 16 x 16 x 1¼-in. (40 x 40 x 3 cm)

Sewing machine

Basic sewing kit (see page 129)

Matching and contrasting sewing threads

1 Following the instructions on page 138, insert a 12-in. (30-cm) zipper between the two 17 x 1¾-in. (43 x 4.5-cm) strips of fabric.

2 With right sides together, aligning the raw edges, pin and stitch a 17 x 2½-in. (43 x 6-cm) strip of fabric to each short end of the zipped panel.

Skill level: 🧵🧵

Sewing time: 1½ hours

Take ⅝-in. (1.5-cm) seam allowances unless otherwise stated.

3 With right sides together, aligning the raw edges, pin the zipped strip to the 17 x 34½-in. (43 x 86-cm) main panel, centering the middle of the zipped strip on the top edge of the main panel. Stitch together along the top edges of the main panel, stopping level with the top and bottom of the zipper.

4 Working one side at a time, pin and stitch the raw long edges of the strips to the main panel, stopping your stitching ⅝ in. (1.5 cm) before you reach the end of each strip.

5 Then fold the bottom half of the main panel up, pin it to the other edge of the zipped strip and to the side strips, and stitch in place. To turn the corners with ease, snip into the fabric twice by about ⅜ in. (1 cm). Before attaching the last side, open the zipper by about 2 in. (5 cm) so as to be able to turn the cover right side out.

Tip As the saying goes, "measure twice and cut once." For this project, you really want to remember that precision is key. Before starting the actual sewing, it helps to draw the seam lines on the wrong side of the fabric, ⅝ in. (1.5 cm) in from all the edges of the fabric strips and the main panel.

6 Turn the cover right side out and insert the foam pad.

guest towel

French elegance is all about details. Turn any toweling fabric into a chic guest towel by adding some decorative patterned cotton. Cream and blue tones will be just right to convey the aristocratic style of the Loire valley châteaux.

Skill level: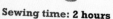

Sewing time: 2 hours

Take ⅝-in. (1.5-cm) seam allowances unless otherwise stated.

You will need

Toweling fabric

Printed cotton fabric

Sewing machine

Basic sewing kit (see page 129)

Matching sewing threads

Tip The handstitching in this project (in step 7) is what takes the most time, but I believe it is worth the effort: the towel will look pretty on both sides.

1 Cut your toweling fabric into a rectangle; the towel can be any size you want. Cut two strips of printed cotton fabric 2 in. (5 cm) wide and the same length as your toweling panel. With right sides together, aligning the long raw edges, pin and stitch one strip to each long side of the toweling panel.

2 Fold over the strips to the wrong side of the panel. Fold under ⅝ in. (1.5 cm), pin, and topstitch about ⅛ in. (3 mm) from the fold.

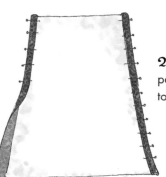

3 On both short sides of the panel, fold over ⅝ in. (1.5 cm) twice to the wrong side. Pin and stitch through all layers, close to the fold. Turn the panel over.

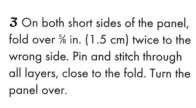

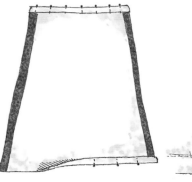

4 Cut a strip of fabric 2 in. (5 cm) wide and twice the combined length and width of the toweling panel plus about 8 in. (20 cm); the extra fabric is to allow for the mitered corners. You may need to join strips together to achieve the right length. Fold both long edges to the wrong side by about ⅜ in. (1 cm) and press.

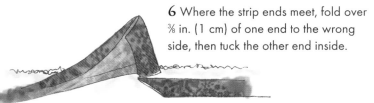

5 Pin the strip to the right side of the toweling panel, ⅜ in. (1 cm) from the edge. To turn the first corner, place a pin ⅜ in. (1 cm) from the edge, fold the strip back on itself (level with the pin), then fold the top edge of the strip back over parallel with the side edge and continue pinning along the second side of the toweling panel.

6 Where the strip ends meet, fold over ⅜ in. (1 cm) of one end to the wrong side, then tuck the other end inside.

7 Slipstitch the cotton strip in place all around, including the mitered corners.

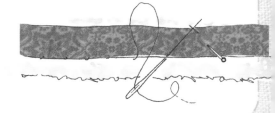

velvet pillow

Like others, I love crisp cotton and bold patterned fabrics during the summer, but prefer the touch of soft velvet and solid colors during the cold season. With its floral embossed velvet and dark silky fabric, this pillow is reminiscent of the formal gardens of the Loire châteaux and the pearl-gray shimmering surface of their sculpted fountains; it is all about luxury and calm.

You will need

One rectangle of plain fabric measuring 12 x 3 in. (31 x 8 cm)

One rectangle of velvet fabric measuring 12 x 3 in. (31 x 8 cm)

One rectangle of plain fabric measuring 12 x 25 in. (31 x 63 cm)

Two strips of velvet fabric measuring 2½ x 29 in. (6.5 x 73 cm)

One rectangle of plain fabric measuring 12 x 2 in. (31 x 5 cm)

10-in. (25-cm) closed-end zipper

14-in. (35-cm) square pillow form (cushion pad)

Sewing machine

Basic sewing kit (see page 129)

Matching sewing threads

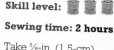

Skill level:

Sewing time: 2 hours

Take ⅝-in. (1.5-cm) seam allowances unless otherwise stated.

1 With right sides together, aligning the raw edges, pin and machine stitch the two 12 x 3-in. (31 x 8-cm) rectangles together along one long side. Lay the 12 x 25-in. (31 x 63-cm) rectangle wrong side down on your work surface. Place the rectangles previously assembled on top, right sides together, aligning the raw edges of the velvet fabric and of the plain fabric. Pin and stitch together. Press the seams open.

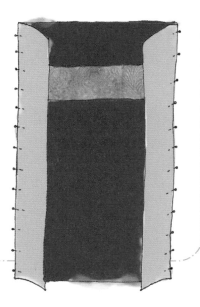

2 Place the main panel right side up on your work surface. Pin one 2½ x 29-in. (6.5 x 73-cm) strip of velvet fabric right side down along each long side. Machine stitch and press the seams open.

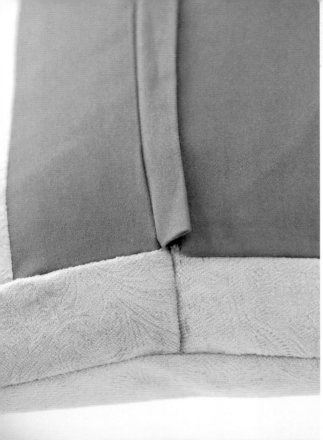

3 The 12 x 2-in. (31 x 5-cm) strip of fabric will be used as a flap to hide the zipper. Along both short sides, fold over ⅝ in. (1.5 cm) to the wrong side and press. Fold the whole strip in half lengthwise.

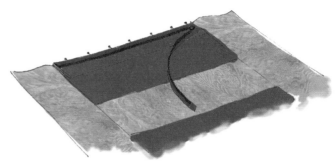

4 Lay the main panel right side up on your work surface. Lay the flap along the center of the short edge of the panel with the velvet strip, aligning the raw edges. Place the zipper right side down on top, aligning the edge of the zipper tape with the raw edges of the flap. Pin all three layers together.

5 Using a zipper foot, machine stitch along the edge to secure both the flap and zipper, keeping your stitching close to the teeth. Press the seam so that the flap covers the zipper.

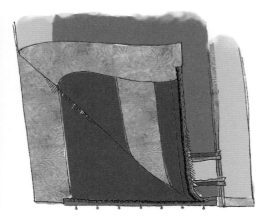

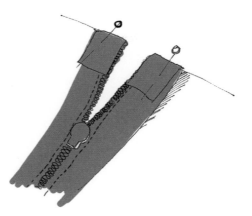

6 Fold the other short edge of the panel up to meet the first short edge, right sides together, and pin the other side of the zipper tape to it. Machine stitch in place, keeping your stitching close to the zipper teeth.

7 Fold over the ends of the zipper tape and hand stitch in place, keeping your stitching close to the teeth.

8 With right sides together, aligning the raw edges, pin and machine stitch across the width of the velvet strips, in line with the stitching that holds the zipper in place to form the panel into a tube.

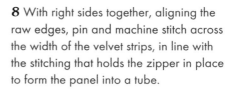

9 With right sides together, align the edges of the cushion, making sure that the velvet rectangle parallel to the zipper lies ¾ in. (2 cm) short of the top. Secure with pins. Before placing the last pins, unzip the zipper by about 1 in. (3 cm). Machine stitch together on both sides. Trim the seam allowances a little. Turn right side out and insert the pillow form (cushion pad).

honeycomb bathrobe

Indulge in "*la vie de château*" with this sophisticated honeycomb bathrobe—just perfect to wear after a relaxing bath or just to enjoy a slow morning. It is shorter than usual to keep the style spruce and neat. It is presented in three different sizes and, thanks to the printed cotton details, can be personalized to your family members' tastes. It also makes a great gift!

You will need

1⅜ yd (125 cm) honeycomb (cotton waffle) fabric, 55–60 in. (140–150 cm) wide

12 in. (30 cm) printed cotton fabric, 55–60 in. (140–150 cm) wide

Pattern pieces A, B, C from pull-out pattern sheet

Sewing machine

Basic sewing kit (see page 129)

Tracing paper and pencil

Matching sewing threads

Water-soluble pen or tailor's chalk

Tip To make the bathrobe longer, simply increase the length of the front and back pieces. If the fabric you wish to use is 36 or 44 in. (90 or 112 cm) wide, you will need at least 2½ yards (2.2 meters) of fabric.

1 Place tracing paper on top of the pattern sheet and trace off pattern pieces A, B, and C in your chosen size (S, M, or L). Cut out the pieces.

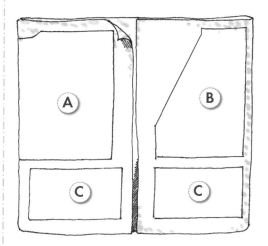

(A) Back: cut one on fold
(B) Front: cut two
(C) Sleeve: cut four

Skill level: 🧵🧵

Sewing time: 3 hours

Take ⅝-in. (1.5-cm) seam allowances unless otherwise stated.

2 With right sides together, fold the honeycomb fabric in three, bringing the selvages (selvedges) together at the center. Pin the pattern pieces on the fabric, following the layout guide; note that the back has to be pinned on the fold. All seam allowances are included, so all you need to do is to trace the pattern pieces onto the fabric with a water-soluble pen or tailor's chalk and cut the fabric along those marks.

3 Zigzag stitch or serge (overlock) all raw edges to prevent the fabric from fraying.

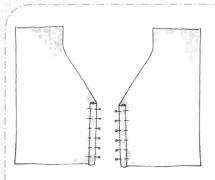
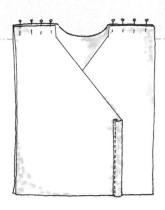
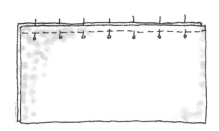

4 On the straight center edges below the V-shaped neckline, fold over 1 in. (2.5 cm) and then another 1 in. (2.5 cm) to the wrong side and press. Pin and stitch close to the fold.

5 Place the back piece wrong side down on your work surface. Lay the two front pieces on top, right sides together, aligning the shoulder edges. Pin and stitch both layers. Press the seam open.

6 Take two sleeve pieces. With right sides together, aligning the edges, pin together along one long edge, then machine stitch. Repeat with the other two sleeve pieces. Press the seam open.

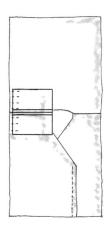
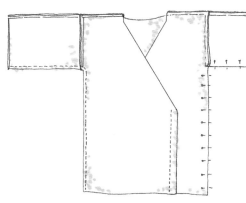
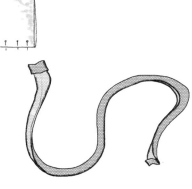

7 Place the bathrobe flat on your work surface, right side up. With right sides together, aligning the edges, place one sleeve on top, making sure the sleeve seam made in step 6 aligns with the shoulder seam made in step 5. Pin and stitch together. Repeat on the other side with the other sleeve. Press the seam allowances toward the sleeves.

8 With right sides together, aligning the zigzagged or serged (overlocked) edges on the left-hand side of the bathrobe, pin and stitch together the front, back, and sleeve to form a single seam from the end of the sleeve to the hemline. Press the seams open. Repeat on the right-hand side of the bathrobe. Hem the bathrobe by folding over ⅝ in. (1.5 cm) twice to the wrong side. Pin and stitch all layers.

9 For the neckline trim, cut a strip of printed cotton fabric 2 in. (5 cm) wide and the required length for the size you are making: 40 in./102 cm (S), 44 in./112 cm (M), or 48 in./ 122 cm (L). Zigzag stitch or serge (overlock) the long edges to prevent the fabric from fraying. Fold the short edges over to the wrong side by ⅝ in. (1.5 cm). Fold in two lengthwise, wrong sides together.

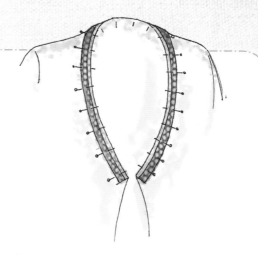

10 Pin this strip of fabric around the neckline of the bathrobe, aligning the zigzagged or serged (overlocked) edges. Pin and stitch all layers ⅜ in. (1 cm) from the edge. Press the seam allowance. Press the neckline trim away from the honeycomb fabric so that it stands up. On the right side, topstitch the honeycomb fabric ¹⁄₁₆ in. (2 mm) from the seamline.

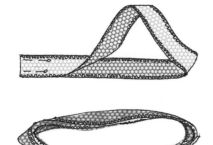

11 Cut two 20 x 2-in. (51 x 5-cm) strips of printed cotton fabric. Zigzag stitch or serge (overlock) both long edges of each strip. With right sides together, pin and stitch the short sides of one strip together to form a loop. Repeat with the other strip. Press the seams open. Fold the loops in two lengthwise, wrong sides together.

12 Aligning the zigzagged or serged (overlocked) edges, pin and stitch one loop to one sleeve. Repeat on the other side. Fold the printed fabric back along the stitching line and press the seam allowances toward the honeycomb fabric.

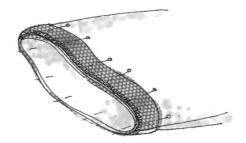

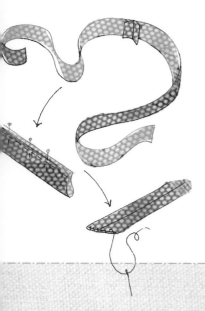

13 To make the belt, cut one 4 x 55-in. (10 x 140-cm) strip and one 4 x 16-in. (10 x 40-cm) strip in cotton fabric. With right sides together, pin and stitch them together along one of their short sides. Press the seam open. Fold the strip in two lengthwise, right sides together, aligning the raw edges, then pin and stitch along the long raw edge, leaving a 4-in. (10-cm) gap for turning. Press the seam open and turn right side out. Center the seam widthwise and press. Fold the short sides over to the inside by ⅝ in. (1.5 cm) and topstitch them ¹⁄₁₆ in. (2 mm) from the edge.

bath mat

This bath mat epitomizes the luxury of the Loire castles and the jacquard patterned fabric gives it a discreet touch of elegance. Why not be a little daring? Forget the whites and light colors that are so frequent in the bathroom: for this project I suggest a chic, muted gray color palette.

Skill level:

Sewing time: 2 hours

Take ⅝-in. (1.5-cm) seam allowances unless otherwise stated.

You will need

One 18½ x 31½-in. (47 x 80-cm) rectangle of toweling

One 14 x 31½-in. (35 x 80-cm) rectangle of gray toweling

Two 3½ x 31½-in. (9 x 80-cm) strips of jacquard patterned fabric

Two 2½ x 31½-in. (6 x 80-cm) strips of gray fabric

Sewing machine

Basic sewing kit (see page 129)

Matching sewing threads

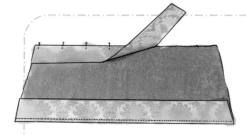

1 With right sides together, aligning the raw edges, pin and machine stitch one jacquard strip along each long side of the 14 x 31½-in. (35 x 80-cm) rectangle of toweling. Trim the seam allowances and press the seams open.

2 Fold the long sides of the 2½ x 31½-in. strips of gray fabric to the wrong side by ⅝ in. (1.5 cm) and press. Lay the strips right side up on the right side of the panel from step one, centering them over the seam lines in order to conceal them. Topstitch the strips in place, stitching close to the edges.

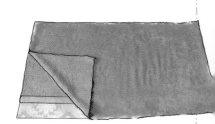

3 Place the panel from steps 1 and 2 right side up on your work surface. Place the 18½ x 31½-in. (47 x 80-cm) rectangle of toweling on top, right side down, aligning the raw edges. Pin and machine stitch together, leaving a 6-in. (15-cm) opening in one short side. Trim the seam allowances, turn right side out, and press.

4 Using a needle and thread, slipstitch the opening closed (see page 133).

guestbook cover

With its rich silver shine, this guestbook cover is in keeping with the traditional grandeur of the Loire valley châteaux: it definitely attracts the eye, while remaining sophisticated and elegant. Instructions are given to suit any size of notebook. You could even make a cover for your favorite novel or coffee-table book.

Skill level:

Sewing time:

1½ hours

Take ⅝-in. (1.5-cm) seam allowances unless otherwise stated.

You will need

Notebook

Silver-patterned fabric (see box to calculate amount)

Sewing machine

Basic sewing kit (see page 129)

Matching sewing threads

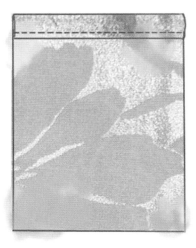

1 Along the top edge of the pocket panel, fold over ¼ in. (5 mm) to the wrong side and press. Repeat once more and press again, then machine stitch close to the fold.

How to measure and cut your fabric

Outer and lining panels Measure your notebook and make a note of the height of the notebook and the combined width of the front and back covers and spine. Add 1½ in. (3.5 cm) to the height and the same amount to the combined width. Cut two panels to this size.

Inner flaps Measure and make a note of the height of the cover and two-thirds of the width of the cover. Add 1½ in. (3.5 cm) to the height and cut two panels to this size.

Inner pocket Cut one piece the same width and about two-thirds of the height of the inner flaps.

2 Place one inner flap right side up on your work surface. Place the pocket panel right side up on top. Along the long right-hand side, fold over ⅜ in. (1 cm) of both layers to the wrong side and press. Pin and machine stitch both layers close to the raw edges.

3 Place the other inner flap right side up on your work surface. Along the long left-hand side, fold over ⅜ in. (1 cm) to the wrong side and press. Pin and machine stitch close to the raw edge (wrong side shown).

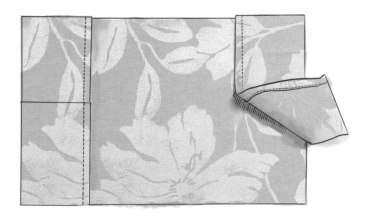

4 Place the lining panel right side up on your work surface, with the short edges to the sides. Place the inner flaps right side up on top, aligning the raw edges on the right- and left-hand sides.

5 Place the outer panel on top, right sides together, aligning the raw edges. Pin and machine stitch all around, leaving a 3-in. (7.5-cm) opening in one side. Trim the seam allowances and clip the corners, then turn right side out and press.

6 With a thread and needle, slipstitch the opening closed (see page 133).

flowerpot cover

A potted flower or plant is a simple gift that is always appreciated. If you have a little extra time, how about adding a personal touch by making this elegant flowerpot cover? Using a richly embroidered fabric will turn your gift into a very classy offering.

You will need

Two 19 x 8-in. (48 x 20-cm) rectangles of heavyweight fabric

Template on page 139

One 7 x 14-in. (18 x 36-cm) rectangle of heavyweight fabric

Sewing machine

Basic sewing kit (see page 129)

Matching sewing threads

This flowerpot cover is for pots up to 5¼ in. (13 cm) in diameter.

Skill level:

Sewing time: 1½ hours

Take ⅝-in. (1.5-cm) seam allowances unless otherwise stated.

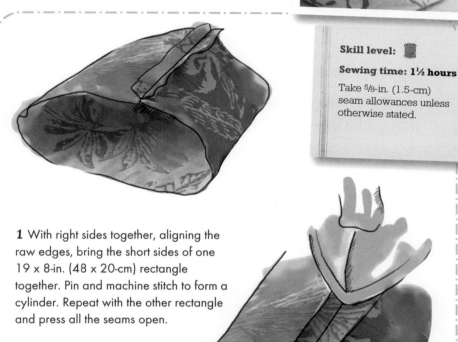

1 With right sides together, aligning the raw edges, bring the short sides of one 19 x 8-in. (48 x 20-cm) rectangle together. Pin and machine stitch to form a cylinder. Repeat with the other rectangle and press all the seams open.

2 Using the template on page 139, cut two circles of fabric from the 7 x 14-in. (18 x 36-cm) square of heavyweight fabric.

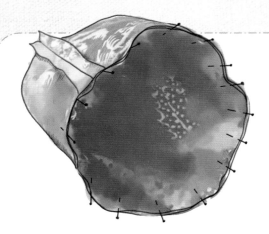

3 With right sides together, pin and machine stitch one circle to one cylinder end. Repeat with the other cylinder and circle. Trim the seam allowances and press the seams open.

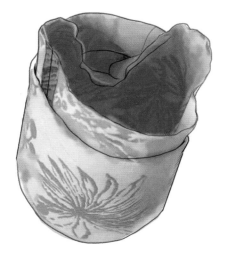

4 Turn one cylinder right side out. Insert the other cylinder inside it, with wrong sides together. Fold 1¼ in. (3 cm) over to the wrong side along the top of the outer cylinder, so that the raw edge lies between the outer and the inner pieces.

5 Around the top edge of the inner cylinder, fold down ⅝ in. (1.5 cm) and then another ⅝ in. (1.5 cm), so that the edge lies over the outer cylinder. Pin in place, then slipstitch all around.

Tip This project can be adapted to store various objects: pegs in the laundry room, toy figurines in a kid's bedroom, cotton balls in the bathroom, and so on.

à la campagne

Old-world, authentic, simple, and natural:
these few words define French country
style. Here's how to achieve this seemingly
effortless look.

table runner

Red stripes and checks are very common in traditional French kitchens. In combination with ecru and taupe, they will add warmth and authenticity to any dining table. To stay true to the subdued country style, a touch is enough! A table runner is a great project for this bold traditional print.

You will need

One 60 x 6-in. (150 x 15-cm) rectangle of striped fabric

Two 60 x 6-in. (150 x 15-cm) rectangles of checked fabric

Two 15½ x 6-in. (39 x 15-cm) rectangles of checked fabric

Sewing machine

Basic sewing kit (see page 129)

Matching sewing threads

Tip For this project, I recommend using fabric that is 60 in. (150 cm) wide: you'll use the full width and have few scraps.

1 Zigzag or serge (overlock) all sides of the 60 x 6-in. (150 x 15-cm) rectangle of striped fabric, both long sides and one short side of each 60 x 6-in. (150 x 15 cm) rectangle of checked fabric, and one long side of each 15½ x 6-in. (39 x 15-cm) rectangle of checked fabric.

Skill level:

Sewing time: 1½ hours

Take ⅝-in. (1.5-cm) seam allowances unless otherwise stated.

2 With right sides together, aligning the long zigzagged or serged (overlocked) edges, pin and machine stitch the three 60 x 6-in. (150 x 15-cm) strips together, placing the striped fabric in the middle. Press the seams open.

3 Place the panel right side facing up on your work surface. With right sides together, aligning the zigzagged or serged (overlocked) edges, pin one 15½ x 6-in. (39 x 15-cm) rectangle to one short end of the panel and machine stitch. Repeat on the opposite side, using the second 15½ x 6-in. (39 x 15-cm) rectangle. Press the seams open.

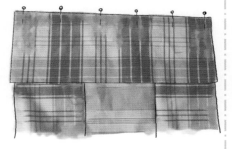

4 Turn under ⅜ in. (1 cm) to the wrong side all around to form a hem and pin in place, mitering the corners (see page 137). Machine stitch.

nap mat

Folded in two and rolled up, this nap mat is convenient and handy. You can carry it to the garden or use it as an extra mat for a child's sleepover. It is made from ticking—a traditional heavyweight fabric that was originally used to make mattresses. Nowadays, very few mattresses are still covered with ticking. However, I like to keep the original use in mind when working with vintage prints, so a nap mat seemed appropriate! The project also takes advantage of the full width of the ticking (102 in./260 cm) and leaves no scraps.

You will need

20 in. (50 cm) ticking, 102 in. (260 cm) wide

Two 55-in. (140-cm) lengths of white grosgrain (petersham) ribbon, 1¼–1½ in. (3–4 cm) wide

18 x 47½ in. (46 x 121 cm) thick batting (wadding)

Sewing machine

Basic sewing kit (see page 129)

Matching sewing threads

Walking foot for sewing machine (optional)

Skill level:

Sewing time: 2 hours

Take ⅝-in. (1.5-cm) seam allowances unless otherwise stated.

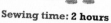

1 Cut 4 in. (10 cm) off the short side of your ticking panel to obtain a 4 x 20-in (10 x 50-cm) strip. Cut this strip into two 4 x 10-in. (10 x 25-cm) rectangles. Cut the remaining ticking in half widthwise to give two 49 x 20-in. (125 x 50-cm) panels.

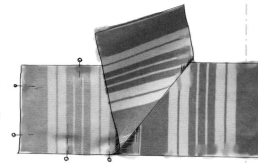

2 To make the handle, place the two 4 x 10-in. (10 x 25-cm) strips right sides together, aligning the raw edges. Cut off ⅝ in. (1.5 cm) from both short sides. Pin and stitch all around, leaving a 3-in. (7.5-cm) opening along one long side. Snip off the corners, turn right side out, and press.

3 Topstitch along the long sides, close to the edge.

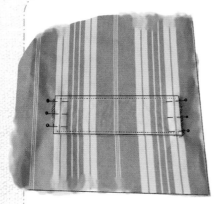

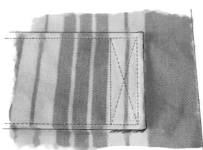

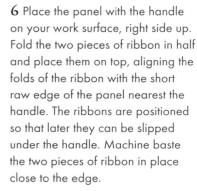

4 Place one of the main 49 x 20-in. (125 x 50-cm) panels right side up on your work surface. Place the handle on this panel, about 3½ in. (9 cm) down from one short edge and about 1¼ in. (3 cm) in from one long edge. The print should help you: align the stripes of the handle with the stripes of the panel. Pin the short sides of the handle through all layers.

5 Box stitch each short end of the handle in place.

6 Place the panel with the handle on your work surface, right side up. Fold the two pieces of ribbon in half and place them on top, aligning the folds of the ribbon with the short raw edge of the panel nearest the handle. The ribbons are positioned so that later they can be slipped under the handle. Machine baste the two pieces of ribbon in place close to the edge.

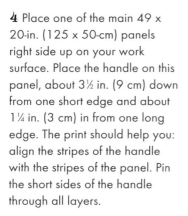

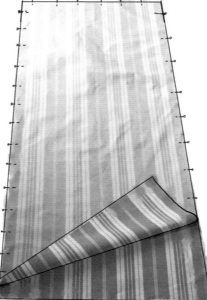

7 With right sides together, pin both panels together and stitch all around, leaving a 9-in. (23-cm) opening on the short side opposite the handle. Turn right side out.

Tip If the batting (wadding) is thick and high in density, you may want to use a walking foot for the final step of this project.

8 Slip the batting (wadding) inside and slipstitch the opening closed.

9 With tailor's chalk, draw a line dividing the mat in two lengthwise. Pin to prevent the batting (wadding) from moving around, and topstitch along the line.

bed runner

To make this bed runner, select a textured fabric in a cream or ecru tone to convey a sense of comfort and serenity; for an authentic French feel, we used matelassé fabric (a woven fabric that appears to be padded or quilted and looks rather like a traditional French *boutis*). The rounded corners, puffy texture, and pale color of this echo both the soft, whitewashed walls and the embroidered vintage linen that are so typical of the French rural tradition.

Skill level: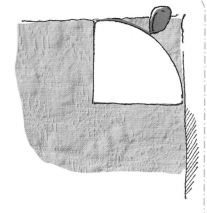

Sewing time: 1 hour

Take ⅝-in. (1.5-cm) seam allowances unless otherwise stated.

You will need

Outer fabric (see box)

Backing fabric (see box)

Piping (see box)

Template on page 141 (photocopy the template at 200% to enlarge it to the correct size)

Sewing machine

Basic sewing kit (see page 129)

Matching sewing threads

1 With the wrong side of the fabric facing you, lay the photocopied template on one corner of the outer fabric and draw around the rounded corner with tailor's chalk, a pencil, or a fadeaway fabric marker pen. Repeat on the other three corners, then cut along the drawn lines. Mark and cut all four corners of the lining fabric in the same way.

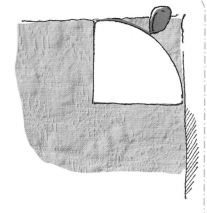

How much fabric?

Measure the width of the bed and decide how far down the sides of the bed you want the runner to go: this gives you the length of the fabric you need to cut. The width of the bed runner is for you to decide, but I recommend anything between 24 and 32 in. (60 and 80 cm). Cut both the outer and the backing fabrics to the same size. The amount of piping needed depends on the size of the bed runner; measure all around your fabric and add about 6 in. (15 cm). Prepare the piping following the instructions on page 136.

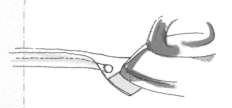

2 Remove 4–5 stitches at one end of the piping and cut about 1 in. (3 cm) off the cord. On the same end, fold over about ½ in. (1.5 cm) of the fabric covering the cord and press.

3 Lay the outer fabric wrong side down on your work surface. Place the piping on top, aligning the raw edges. Pin all around. Where both ends of the piping meet, insert the uncut end of the cord into the folded end of the fabric. Using a zipper foot and a long stitch, machine stitch the outer fabric and the piping together, keeping your stitching as close to the cord as possible. Remove the pins.

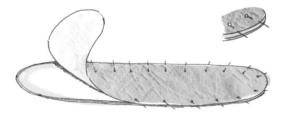

4 Lay the backing fabric on top of the outer fabric, right sides together, aligning the raw edges. The piping is sandwiched between the two panels of fabric. Pin and machine stitch all layers together, leaving an 8-in. (20-cm) opening in one side. On the curved corners, snip into the seam allowance (see page 132).

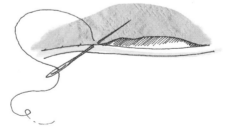

5 Turn the bed runner right side out. Fold the excess fabric inside the opening and pin. Hand stitch carefully and press the bed runner.

baguette bag

Many French idiomatic expressions refer to bread: *ne pas manger de ce pain là* ("I won't eat that kind of bread," meaning I won't have to do anything with it), *ça ne mange pas de pain* ("no need to feed it bread," meaning it does not cost anything), *avoir du pain sur la planche* ("to have bread on one's board," meaning to have a lot on one's plate), and so on. We French have a love affair with bread. A drawstring bag can be found in many French kitchens to keep the daily baguettes fresh—so go ahead and make this project for your own kitchen!

You will need

Two 30 x 9-in. (76 x 23-cm) rectangles of striped fabric

45 in. (114 cm) beige cord, approx. ¼ in. (5 mm) in diameter

Sewing machine

Basic sewing kit (see page 129)

Matching sewing threads

Skill level: 🧵

Sewing time: 1 hour

Take ⅝-in. (1.5-cm) seam allowances unless otherwise stated.

1 Treat all raw edges of both rectangles of fabric to prevent fraying, using pinking shears, a zigzag stitch, or serging (overlocking).

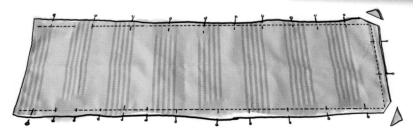

2 With right sides together, aligning the edges and the printed stripes, pin the rectangles of fabric together along one short side and both long sides. Measuring 2¾ in. (7 cm) from the unpinned short side, make a mark on both long sides with tailor's chalk or a water-soluble pencil. Measure 1½ in. (4 cm) from these marks and make another mark. Stitch around the three pinned sides, interrupting your stitching between the marks. Clip the corners and press the seams open.

Tip Be sure to use a fabric that will withstand high temperatures, as you will have to wash the bag regularly.

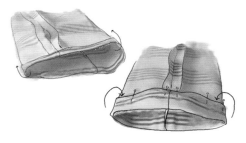

3 Along the top edge, fold over ⅝ in. (1.5 cm) to the wrong side and press. Fold over another 1¾ in. (4.5 cm), forming a channel to thread the cord through. Pin and stitch close to the bottom of the folded-over fabric. Turn the bag right side out.

4 Cut the cord in half. Attach a safety pin to one end of one cord. Feed the cord into the opening on the left-hand side of the bag and all the way around the channel until it comes out at the left-hand side again. Repeat with the other cord on the right-hand side of the bag.

5 Knot the two ends of cord on each side in a double knot. If necessary, to prevent the cord from fraying, wrap the same color of thread around the rope end several times, pull tight, and secure with a couple of knots. Repeat on all four cord ends.

hot water bottle cover

The old-world character of a French country house is about elegance and comfort. With the fireplace situated in the kitchen or in the living room, bedrooms are often cooler: don't forget to fill a hot water bottle for your family or guests! To warm up in style, make this cover in a delicate floral print, to tone in with the natural colors of the bucolic surroundings.

Skill level:

Sewing time: 1½ hours

Take ⅝-in. (1.5-cm) seam allowances unless otherwise stated.

You will need

Pattern pieces D, E, F from pull-out pattern sheet

20 x 24 in. (51 x 61 cm) floral mediumweight fabric

30 in. (76 cm) satin ribbon, ¼ in. (7 mm) wide

Two popper snaps

Sewing machine

Basic sewing kit (see page 129)

Matching sewing threads

Safety pin

1 Using pattern pieces D, E, and F, cut one back, one top front piece, and one bottom front piece. All seam allowances are included, so all you need to do is to trace the template pieces onto the fabric with a water-soluble pen or tailor's chalk and cut the fabric along those marks.

2 Fold over the long, straight edge of the top front piece to the wrong side by ⅜ in. (1 cm) twice and press. Machine stitch close to the fold. Repeat with the top edge of the bottom front piece.

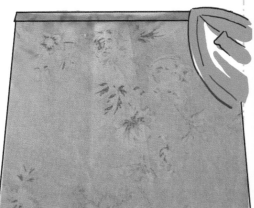

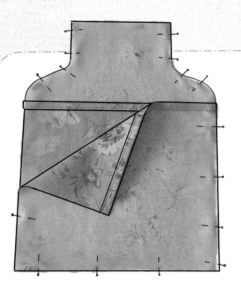

3 Place the back piece on your work surface, right side up. Place the top front piece right side down on top, aligning the raw edges. Then place the bottom front piece right side down on top, again aligning the raw edges; the two front pieces should overlap slightly. Pin and machine stitch all around, leaving the short top edge open.

4 Trim the seam allowances all around to just ³⁄₁₆ in. (5 mm). Serge (overlock) or zigzag stitch the seam allowances together to prevent wear. Turn right side out and press well.

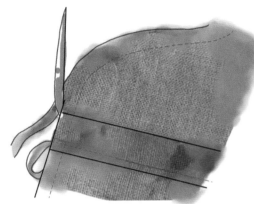

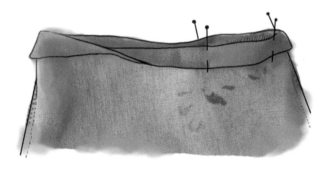

5 Turn the cover wrong side out again and fold over the top edge twice by ³⁄₈ in. (1 cm). Pin in place and press. Machine stitch close to the fold. Turn right side out.

6 Cut a 9½ x 1½-in. (24.5 x 4-cm) strip of fabric. Fold the short ends over to the wrong side by ³⁄₈ in. (1 cm) and press. Fold over the long sides to the middle and press.

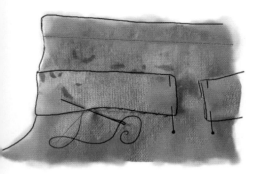

7 Wrap the strip around the neck of the hot water bottle cover, bringing both short ends to the center of the front. Pin and then slipstitch it in place to form a channel, stitching along both long edges of the strip and making sure that you only stitch through one layer of the cover.

8 Attach a safety pin to one end of the ribbon. Feed the ribbon through one of the openings, all around the channel and out of the other opening, making sure the same amount of ribbon overhangs at both ends. Remove the safety pin.

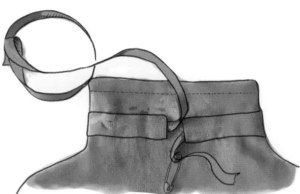

9 Attach two pairs of popper snaps to the overlapping front pieces, making sure that you only stitch through the hem folds so that your stitches are invisible.

bon appétit bolster

A small bolster is a decorative piece that can go in almost any room. Making it in a heavyweight linen fabric is sure to give the piece a traditional rustic feel. I used a beautiful pure linen fabric with "*bon appétit*" woven into it: sober yet elegant. The flat ends are also very typical of French style.

Skill level:

Sewing time: 1½ hours

Take ⅝-in. (1.5-cm) seam allowances unless otherwise stated.

You will need

One 20⅞ x 17¾-in. (53 x 45-cm) rectangle of linen

One 2 x 20⅞-in. (5 x 53-cm) strip of red cotton fabric

One 16 x 8-in. (40 x 20-cm) rectangle of red cotton fabric

Template on page 140

Polyester toy filling

Sewing machine

Basic sewing kit (see page 129)

Matching sewing threads

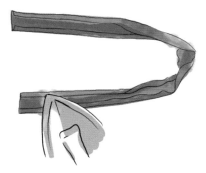

1 With wrong sides together, aligning the raw edges, fold the 20⅞ x 17¾-in. (53 x 45-cm) linen rectangle in two lengthwise. Pin and machine stitch along the long raw edge. Press the seam open and turn right side out.

2 Fold the long sides of the long red strip over to the wrong side by ⅜ in. (1 cm) and press.

Tip The beautiful French linen that I used has "*bon appétit*" woven into it. If you have trouble finding such fabric, you could use lettering stencils and fabric paint to make your own.

3 Place the linen panel on your work surface, with the seam facing you. Lay the red strip from step 2 on top of the seam, centering it so as to conceal it. Slipstitch the strip to the bolster. Since you are working on a piece in the form of a thin tube, be careful not to stitch through the opposite linen layer. When you are done, turn the bolster wrong side out.

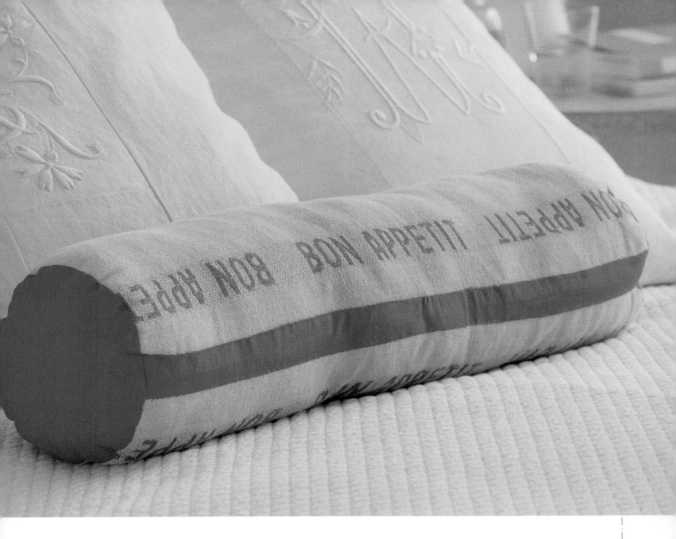

4 Use the template on page 140 to cut two circles from the 16 x 8-in. (40 x 20-cm) rectangle of red fabric. Right sides together, pin one circle to one end of the bolster, and machine stitch in place. Snip the seam allowance. Attach the other circle to the other end of the bolster in the same way, leaving a 6-in. (15-cm) gap in the stitching. Turn the bolster right side out.

5 Stuff the bolster and close opening with a thread and needle using small stitches.

linen drape

Drapes can determine the tone of the whole room and this design, in which linen blends beautifully with twill ribbon, sums up French country style. Also, the flat fell seam technique used here allows you to make a multi-panel, single-layered curtain that looks pretty on both sides.

You will need

55 in. (140 cm) taupe linen, 60 in. (150 cm) wide

16 in. (40 cm) white linen, 60 in. (150 cm) wide

16 in. (40 cm) cream linen 60 in. (150 cm) wide

10 yards (9 m) twill ribbon, ¾ in. (2 cm) wide

Sewing machine

Basic sewing kit (see page 129)

Matching sewing threads

1 Cut the taupe linen into two pieces: one 8 x 60-in. (20 x 150-cm) strip and one 47 x 60-in. (120 x 150-cm) rectangle. Cut the white linen into two equal pieces to give two 8 x 60-in. (20 x 150-cm) strips. Repeat with the cream linen.

2 With right sides together, aligning the raw edges, pin and machine stitch one white strip to each long side of the taupe strip, taking a ¾-in. (2-cm) seam allowance. With right sides together, aligning the raw edges, pin and machine stitch one 8 x 60-in. (20 x 150-cm) cream strip to the right-hand white strip, again taking a ¾-in. (2-cm) seam allowance. Press all the seams open.

Skill level: 🧵🧵

Sewing time: 3½ hours

Take ⅝-in. (1.5-cm) seam allowances unless otherwise stated.

Finished size The fabric amounts given below will make a drape that is approx. 72 in. (183 cm) wide and 58 in. (148 cm) tall. Of course, you can adapt it to your own window size. The finished drape needs to be 1½ to 2 times wider than the window. The finished length depends on the style you are aiming for and the position of the pole above the window. Generally, you'll want to measure from the bottom of the pole to the windowsill and add about 6 in. (15 cm) to your fabric panels.

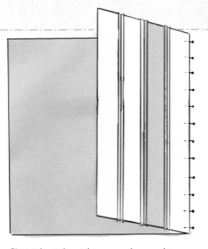

3 With right sides together, taking a ¾-in. (2-cm) seam allowance, pin and machine stitch the taupe 47 x 60-in. (120 x 150-cm) rectangle to the long raw white edge of the panel made in step 2. Press the seam open.

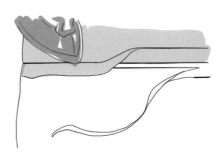

4 Treat all four seams using the flat fell technique. Working on the wrong side of the panel, trim away ⅝ in. (1.5 cm) of each white seam allowance. Press the untrimmed taupe seam allowance toward the trimmed side.

5 Fold the wider, untrimmed seam allowance under until the folded edge meets the seam line. Press, pin, and stitch close to the fold.

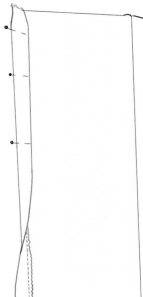

6 Working on the right side of the drape, place a 60-in. (150-cm) strip of twill ribbon along the cream right-hand edge. Pin and stitch very close to the ribbon edge. Turn the ribbon over to the wrong side of the drape and topstitch close to the ribbon edge. Repeat on the left-hand side of the drape.

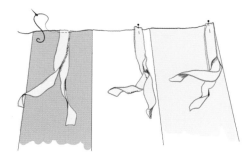

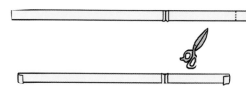

8 Take the remaining 8 x 60-in. (20 x 150-cm) cream strip and cut it in two lengthwise to give two 4 x 60-in. (10 x 150-cm) strips. With right sides together, pin and stitch the two strips together along one short side. Press the seam open. Cut this long strip to fit the width of the curtain panel plus 1½ in. (4 cm). Fold over ¾ in. (2 cm) to the wrong side at each short side and press.

7 With tailor's chalk or a water-soluble fabric marker pen, make ten marks about 8 in. (20 cm) apart along the top edge of curtain, beginning and ending at the sides. Cut twenty 12-in. (30-cm) strips of twill ribbon. Pin two strips at each mark, aligning one end of each pair to the raw edge of the fabric panel. Baste (tack) the ribbons in place, then remove the pins.

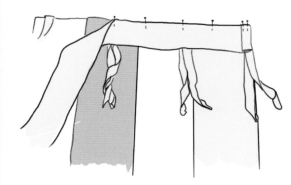

9 Place the panel right side up on your work surface. Place the cream strip from step 8 right side down on top, sandwiching the pairs of twill ribbon in between. Pin and machine stitch through all layers. Fold the strip of fabric over to the wrong side and press. Fold under ⅝ in. (1.5 cm) along the long raw edge of the cream strip, press, and pin in place. Machine stitch close to the fold.

10 To hem the bottom of the drape, turn over a double ¾-in. (2-cm) fold to the wrong side and press. Pin in place, then machine stitch close to the fold.

ruffled garland

Fabric garlands are a smart way to decorate the house for a special event. The combination of fabrics that I've chosen here works particularly well to create an authentically rustic French look, with the roughness of the burlap (hessian) giving some texture to the otherwise soft curves of the ruffles. This garland is also a perfect everyday piece to decorate an old fireplace mantel, a bed frame, or a vintage wooden door.

Skill level: 🧵🧵

Sewing time: 3½ hour

Take ⅝-in. (1.5-cm) seam allowances unless otherwise stated.

You will need

Four 5 x 55-in. (13 x 140-cm) strips of linen fabric

Four 5 x 55-in. (13 x140-cm) strips of burlap (hessian)

Two 4 x 2½-in. (10 x 6-cm) strips of burlap

Two buttons, about 1 in. (2.5 cm) in diameter

Approx. 2¾ yards (2.5 m) matching embroidery floss (thread)

Sewing machine

Basic sewing kit (see page 129)

Matching sewing threads

1 With wrong sides together, aligning the raw edges, stitch the four strips of linen together along their short sides. Press the seams open. Repeat with the four strips of burlap (hessian). Burlap is fragile, so zigzag stitch the seam allowances together to prevent fraying.

Finished size The amounts given above make a garland about 32 in. (80 cm) long; for a longer garland, simply add more fabric. Each new strip will add about 8 in. (20 cm) to the finished length. The precise length depends on the thickness of the weave of the burlap (hessian) and the weight of the linen.

2 Beginning with the short sides, fold over ⅝ in. (1.5 cm) to the wrong side along all sides of the linen panel. Press the folds.

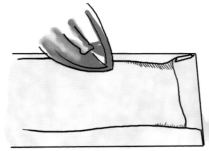

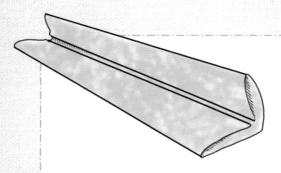

3 Fold the two 4 x 2½-in. (10 x 6-cm) strips of burlap in half lengthwise and press. Fold the long raw edges in to meet at the center crease. Press and stitch close to the fold.

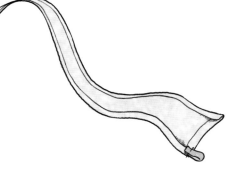

4 Place the linen panel on your work surface, wrong side up. Fold each tie from step 3 in two lengthwise to form a loop. Place one tie at one short side of the linen panel so that it sticks out, aligning it with the bottom long edge. Repeat with the other tie on the opposite short side. Baste (tack) the ties in place.

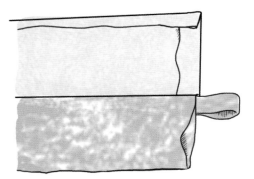

5 Fold over ⅝ in. (1.5 cm) to the wrong side on both short sides of the burlap panel and press. With wrong sides together, aligning the raw edges, fold the burlap panel in two lengthwise. Place the raw edges over the bottom edge of the linen panel, aligning with the tops of the ties.

6 Fold the top edge of the linen panel down over the long raw edges of the burlap. Pin all along and topstitch using a zigzag stitch.

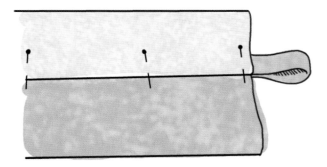

7 Thread an embroidery needle with 2¾ yards (2.5 m) of embroidery floss (thread). Tie a knot at the end and sew a button to one short side, aligning it with the tie.

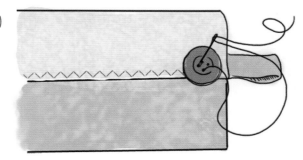

8 Work a line of running stitches about 1 in. (2.5 cm) long along the full length of the garland, inserting the needle into the burlap just below the linen. Pull gently on the embroidery floss (thread) as you stitch along to form ruffles.

9 When you reach the opposite end of the garland, pull the floss and distribute the ruffles evenly. Stitch a second button onto the other short side of the garland. Tie a knot and cut off the excess floss (thread).

CHAPTER 3

la belle Provence

Sunflowers, blue skies, lavender, and cicadas
all speak of sunny Provence. It's time to get
inspired by the relaxed atmosphere of the area
with its traditional prints and the vibrant
color palette...

duvet cover

For this project, we step aside from the traditional bold prints of Provence. The color scheme is more subtle but no less local: taupe for the arid soil, purple for lavender, and pink for fresh roses. The front and back are treated differently to give a more graphic quality to this otherwise very simple and elegant duvet cover.

Skill level: 🧵🧵

Sewing time: 2½ hours

Take ⅝-in. (1.5-cm) seam allowances unless otherwise stated.

You will need

Two strips of purple fabric 5 x 54 in. (13 x 138 cm)

One strip of beige fabric measuring 5 x 54 in. (13 x 138 cm)

One rectangle of beige fabric measuring 21 x 54 in. (53 x 138 cm)

One rectangle of light pink fabric measuring 56 x 54 in. (143 x 138 cm)

One rectangle of light pink fabric measuring 72 x 54 in. (183 x 138 cm)

Sewing machine

Basic sewing kit (see page 129)

Matching sewing threads

This makes a duvet cover measuring 53 x 79 in. (135 x 200 cm)

Tip The only difficulty with this duvet cover is the large amount of fabric you have to work with: you will need to work on a large table.

1 Zigzag stitch or serge (overlock) all raw edges.

2 To make the front of the duvet cover, place one purple strip on top of the 21 x 54-in. (53 x 138-cm) beige rectangle, right sides together. Pin and machine stitch along one long side. With right sides together, pin and machine stitch the 56 x 54-in. (143 cm x 138-cm) light pink rectangle to the other side of the beige rectangle. Press the seams open.

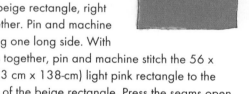
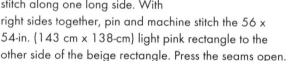
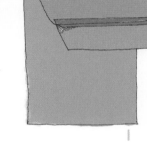

3 To make the back of the duvet cover, with right sides together, place one purple rectangle on top of the 5 x 54-in. (13 x 138-cm) beige rectangle, right sides together. Pin and machine stitch along one long side. With right sides together, pin and machine stitch the 72 x 54-in. (183 x 138-cm) light pink rectangle together to the side of the beige rectangle. Press the seams open.

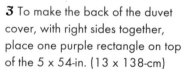
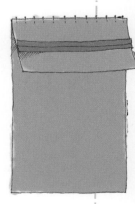

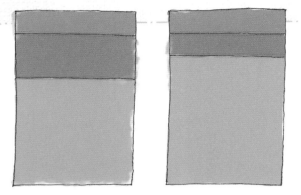

4 Working on the right side of the front, topstitch one line on either side of each seam line, ¼ in. (7 mm) from each seam. Repeat the topstitching on the back of the duvet cover. If you have a twin needle, use it for this step as it will make it much easier to stitch parallel lines: simply position the seam line in between the two needles. Whichever technique you decide on, don't hesitate to mix and match threads.

5 Lay the front of the duvet cover right side up on your work surface, with the back right side down on top, aligning the edges. Pin and machine stitch around the edges of the cover, leaving a 28-in. (70-cm) opening on the short pink side. When you come to a corner, stop ⅝ in. (1.5 cm) from the edge with the needle at its lowest point, then raise the presser foot and pivot the fabric under the needle ready to stitch the next side. Using a slightly shorter stitch here will secure seam lines and prevent premature wear. Trim away excess fabric by clipping the corners (see page 132). Press the seams open.

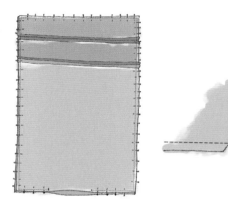

6 Along the opening, fold over the seam allowance to the wrong side. Stitch around the opening within the seam allowance, forming a rectangle. Turn the cover right side out and insert the duvet.

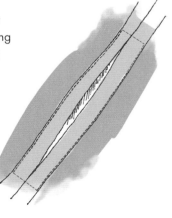

pillowcase

Provence is home to some beautiful Romanesque abbeys. My favorite is the Sénanque abbey, near the village of Gordes: its strict architecture surrounded by beautiful rows of lavender is very soothing. Retain a little of that monastic serenity with this quick and easy project. The topstitching gives it some structure and a light touch of refinement.

Skill level:

Sewing time: 1½ hours

Take ⅝-in. (1.5-cm) seam allowances unless otherwise stated.

You will need

One rectangle of purple fabric measuring 60 x 24 in. (150 x 61 cm)

One rectangle of beige fabric measuring 14 x 24 in. (35 x 61 cm)

Sewing machine

Basic sewing kit (see page 129)

Matching sewing threads

This makes a pillowcase measuring 30 x 20 in. (75 x 50 cm).

1 With right sides together, aligning the raw edges, pin and machine stitch the two rectangles together. Press the seam open. Working on the right side, topstitch one line on either side of the seam line, ¼ in. (7 mm) from the seam. If you have a twin needle, use it for this step as it will make it much easier to stitch parallel lines: simply position the seam line in between the two needles. Whichever technique you decide on, don't hesitate to mix and match threads.

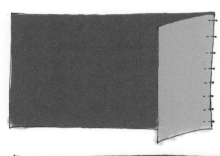

2 On both short sides of the panel, fold over ¼ in. (7 mm) to the wrong side. Repeat, then machine stitch close to the fold.

3 Place the fabric panel right side up on your work surface. With right sides together, fold over the beige rectangle along the seam line. Overlap the other side of the fabric, making sure that the length of the pillowcase when folded is 33 in. (83 cm).

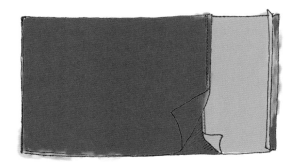

4 Pin and stitch along the raw edges of the pillowcase. Press the seams open, turn right side out, and press again.

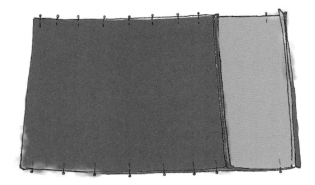

Tip For a really authentic French look, why not make a square 24 x 24-in. (60 x 60-cm) pillowcase?

5 With tailor's chalk or a water-soluble marking pen, draw a rectangle all around the pillowcase, 1½ in. (4 cm) in from the edge. Place several pins within this rectangle to ensure that the pillowcase lies perfectly flat. Using a twin needle and aligning the left needle on the chalk or pencil mark, topstitch along the rectangle. You will not be able to pivot at the corners as you would with a regular needle: instead, raise both foot and twin needle to turn the corners. Slip in the pillow. If you don't have a twin needle, stitch once on the drawn line and once about ⅛ in. (3 mm) from the line.

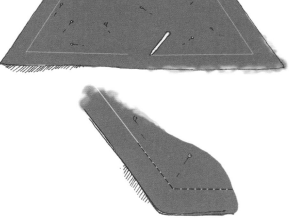

lavender pillow

Lavender is typical of Provence. Harvested at the very end of summer, it is dried, put in small fabric bags, and placed all around the house in cupboards and drawers to deter dust mites. But even natural lavender loses its smell after a few months, so this mini pillow has an inner gauze pouch that lets you replace the lavender when necessary. The outer fabric is in the Provençal mustard yellow that is so reminiscent of the region's sunflower fields.

You will need

One rectangle of Provençal fabric measuring 13½ x 6 in. (34 x 16 cm)

Two 3½-in. (9-cm) squares of gauze (netting)

Sewing machine

Basic sewing kit (see page 129)

Matching sewing threads

Dried lavender

1 On both short sides of the panel of Provençal fabric, fold over ½ in. (1.5 cm) to the wrong side, and press. Repeat, then machine stitch close to the folds.

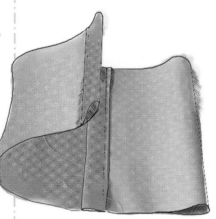

2 Place the fabric panel right side up on your work surface. Fold one short end over by about one-quarter of the length of the panel. Fold the other short side over it, making sure that the length of the mini pillow when folded is 5 in. (13 cm).

3 Pin and stitch along the raw edges of the pillow. Press the seams open, turn right side out, and press again.

4 With tailor's chalk or a water-soluble marking pen, draw a square all around the pillow, 1 in. (2.5 cm) in from the edge. Stitch once on the drawn line and once about ⅛ in. (2 mm) in from the line. Then topstitch all around the pillow, ⅛ in. (2 mm) from the edge.

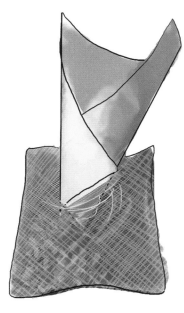

5 Pin and stitch together the two rectangles of gauze (netting), leaving a 1½-in. (4-cm) opening in one side. Snip off the corners and turn right side out.

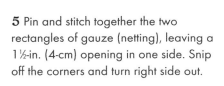

6 Using a piece of paper as a funnel, fill the gauze pouch with dried lavender. Slipstitch the opening closed.

7 Place the lavender pouch inside the mini pillow.

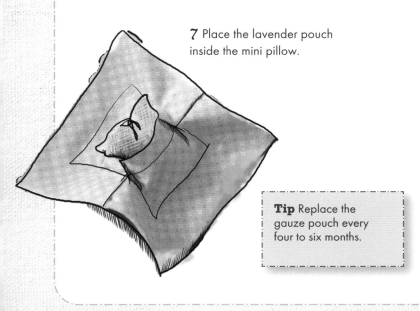

Tip Replace the gauze pouch every four to six months.

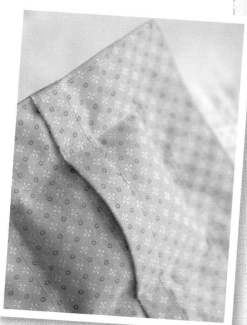

market tote

I love Provençal markets: bright colors, sweet smells, noisy sellers under the warm morning sun. If you ever get a chance to go to Provence, I especially recommend Lourmarin, a town overlooked by a beautiful castle and surrounded by olive tree fields. This market bag will be a great companion for all your market days. Made in a traditional blue and yellow print, it's typically Provençal. It is large with wide handles, so can be carried comfortably. It's also fully reversible.

You will need

Templates on page 141 (photocopy the templates at 200% to enlarge them to the correct size)

18 in. (45 cm) of blue Provençal fabric, 55–60 in. (140–150 cm) wide

18 in. (45 cm) of yellow Provençal fabric, 55–60 in. (140–150 cm) wide

Four 28 x 2¾-in. (71 x 7-cm) strips of blue Provençal fabric

Sewing machine

Basic sewing kit (see page 129)

Tracing paper and pencil

Matching sewing threads

1 Using the photocopied market tote 2 template, cut two blue main panels and two yellow ones. Using the photocopied market tote 1 template, cut two blue bottom pieces and two yellow ones. Cut all 8 pieces on a fold as indicated on the templates.

2 With right sides together, aligning the edges that are the same length, pin and machine stitch each blue main panel to a yellow bottom piece, taking a ⅜-in. (1-cm) seam allowance. Repeat with the yellow main panels and blue bottom pieces. At this point, you should have two blue panels with yellow bottoms and two yellow panels with blue bottoms.

Skill level:

Sewing time: 2 hours

Take ⅝-in. (1.5-cm) seam allowances unless otherwise stated.

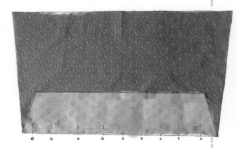

Tip To make a market tote in a single color, simply tape together the photocopied templates, removing the ⅝-in. (1.5-cm) seam allowances between the bottom of the main piece and the top of the bottom piece.

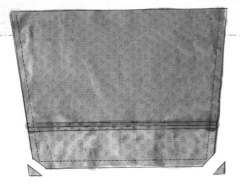

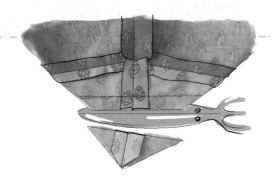

3 Place one panel right side up on your work surface and the matching panel right side down on top, aligning the edges. Pin and machine stitch on three sides, leaving the longest side open. Snip off the corners and press the seams open. Turn right side out. Repeat with the other two panels, but leave a 6-in. (15-cm) gap in the bottom edge. You now have two "flat" totes.

4 Tweak one bottom corner so that about 4 in. (10 cm) of the bottom seam lies in line with the side seam and the corner opens out into a right-angled triangle. Press and pin. Measure 1½ in. (4 cm) from the tip of the triangle and draw a line across the triangle with tailor's chalk or a water-soluble marker pen. Stitch along the line and cut off the excess fabric. Do this on all the bottom corners of both the outer and lining bags.

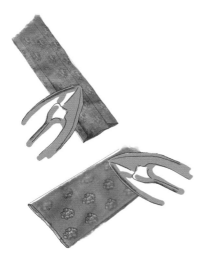

5 To form the handles of the tote, pin one 28 x 2¾-in. (71 x 7-cm) strip on top of the other, right sides together. Pin and stitch along the long sides. Press the seams open. Repeat with the other two strips of fabric. Turn both handles right side out and press, making sure that the seam lines run exactly on the edges. Topstitch the long sides of both handles.

6 Turn the bag with no opening at the bottom right side out. Measure and mark 4 in. (10 cm) from each side seam, then pin the ends of the first handle on the marks. Setting your machine to a long stitch, stitch ⅜ in. (1 cm) from the raw edge. Repeat with the other handle on the other side of the bag.

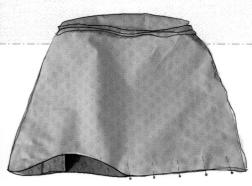

7 Slip the bag with the handles inside the other bag, right sides together, sandwiching the handles between the two layers. Aligning the raw edges and side seams, pin and stitch all around. Press the seams open.

8 Pulling from the opening at the bottom of the outer bag, turn the bag right side out. Press. Pin and topstitch all around the top of the bag.

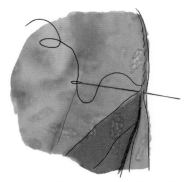

9 Using a needle and thread, slipstitch the opening closed.

french door curtains

French doors provide a great way of letting light into a room. You might occasionally want to obscure the view while keeping the benefit of the window panel: select a lightweight, light-colored fabric, such as this delicate Provençal print, and make your own curtains.

Skill level:

Sewing time: 1½ hours

Take ⅝-in. (1.5-cm) seam allowances unless otherwise stated.

You will need

Printed fabric (see box)

Sewing machine

Basic sewing kit (see page 129)

Adjustable sash (net) curtain rods

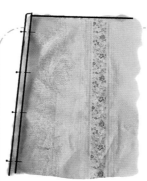

1 Fold over ⅜ in. (1 cm) to the wrong side along the long sides of the two curtain panels and press, then repeat. Pin in place, then machine stitch close to the folds.

2 Cut four strips 4 in. (10 cm) deep x the unhemmed width of the fabric panels. If you are using printed fabric with large motifs, cut the strips to match the design on the panels. Make a double ⅜-in. (1-cm) fold to the wrong side along the short sides of the four strips. Pin and stitch close to the fold.

3 Fold over ⅜ in. (1 cm) to the wrong side along the long sides of the strips and press. Fold the strips in two lengthwise, wrong sides together, and press.

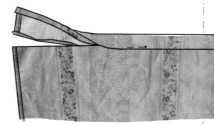

4 Place one curtain panel right side up on your work surface. Place one of the short strips from the previous step over the top raw edge and pin in place ⅜ in. (1 cm) below the raw edge of the curtain panel, thus forming a channel. Topstitch. Repeat at the base of the panel, then treat the second panel in the same way. Finally, insert the curtain rods into the channels.

How much fabric?
Measure one glass panel. Add ¾ in. (2 cm) to the height and 3 in. (8 cm) to the width. Cut two rectangles of fabric to this size—one for each door. If the fabric you select is wide enough, you may be able to get two curtains out of one width of fabric. You will also need four strips of fabric 4 in. (10 cm) deep x the unhemmed width of each curtain.

tablecloth

May and June are the most exquisite months in Provence: the weather is sunny, but mild enough to take full advantage of the outdoors and share meals in the garden. This tablecloth is made in a Provençal print combined with beige and light blue fabrics for a natural, subdued look.

Skill level: 🧵🧵

Sewing time: 2½ hours

Take ⅝-in. (1.5-cm) seam allowances unless otherwise stated.

You will need

One 40-in. (101-cm) square of Provençal fabric

Two 40 x 6-in. (101 x 15-cm) rectangles of beige linen

Two 49½ x 6-in. (125 x 15-cm) rectangles of beige linen

One 53½-in. (135-cm) square of blue cotton fabric for backing

Sewing machine

Basic sewing kit (see page 129)

Matching sewing threads

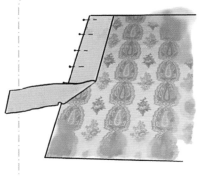

1 With right sides together, aligning the raw edges, pin and machine stitch a 40 x 6-in. (101 x 15-cm) rectangle of beige linen along two opposite sides of the Provençal fabric. Press the seams open.

2 With right sides together, pin and machine stitch one 49½ x 6-in. (125 x 15-cm) rectangle of beige linen to each long edge of the Provençal-and-linen panel. Press the seams open.

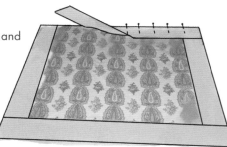

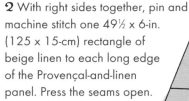

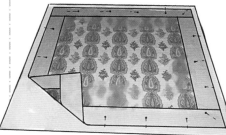

3 Place the 53½-in. (135-cm) blue square right side down on your work surface. Center the Provençal and linen panel right side up on top and pin in place. The blue fabric should overhang the top panel by 2 in. (5 cm) all around.

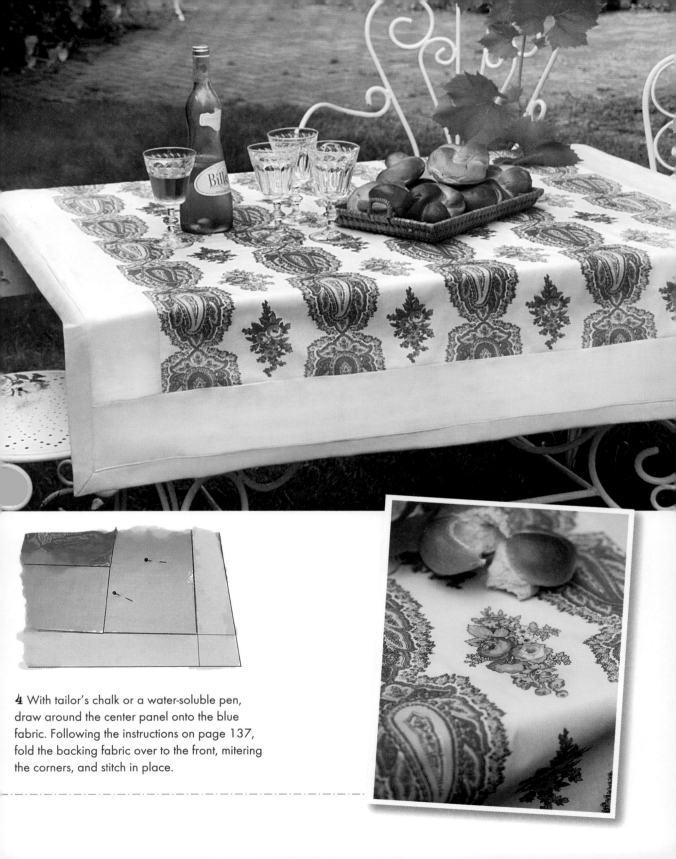

4 With tailor's chalk or a water-soluble pen, draw around the center panel onto the blue fabric. Following the instructions on page 137, fold the backing fabric over to the front, mitering the corners, and stitch in place.

au bord de la mer

From wind-swept Normandy to the breathtaking limestone calanques (inlets) of Mediterranean Provence, French coastal style is varied and playful: let's get sewing!

bottle tote

The traditional stripes of the southwestern region of France known as the Pays Basque are usually irregular and very colorful. This heavyweight fabric is often used for deckchairs, rope-soled sandals, or totes. In this project we decided to use it to make a picnic bottle tote. For sure, it's a very stylish way to bring your fresh lemonade or chilled wine to a beach picnic.

Skill level: 🧵🧵

Sewing time: 1½ hours

Take ⅝-in. (1.5-cm) seam allowances unless otherwise stated.

You will need

Two 8 x 14-in. (20 x 35.5-cm) rectangles of striped fabric

Two 8 x 14-in. (20 x 35.5-cm) rectangles of lining fabric

Two 4½ x 16½-in. (11.5 x 42-cm) strips of striped fabric

Sewing machine

Basic sewing kit (see page 129)

Matching sewing threads

Tip This is also a very special way of wrapping a good bottle of French wine as a gift.

1 Lay one striped rectangle right side up on your work surface and place the second one right side down on top. Pin and machine stitch around three sides, leaving one short side open. Trim seam allowances and snip off the corners. Press the seams open. Repeat with the lining fabric.

2 Fold up the bottom so that the bottom seam lies over one side seam to form a diamond shape. Press and pin. Measure 1⅛ in. (3 cm) up from the base of the diamond and 1⅛ in. (3 cm) down from the tip along the bottom seam. Using tailor's chalk or a water-soluble fabric marker pen, draw two horizontal lines across the diamond at these points. Stitch along each line, then cut off the excess fabric. Repeat with the lining fabric bag.

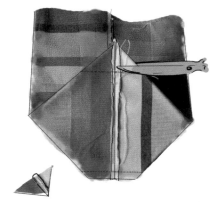

3 Turn the striped bag right side out. On the top raw edge, turn 1½ in. (4 cm) over to the wrong side. Leaving the lining bag wrong side out, turn 1¼ in. (3 cm) over to the wrong side. Insert the lining into the striped fabric bag, matching the side seams. The lining should finish a little short of the top edge.

4 With wrong sides together, aligning the raw edges, fold one 4½ x 16½-in. (11 x 42-cm) strip in half lengthwise. Pin and stitch along the long raw edge. Press the seam open and turn right side out. Centering the seam line on the back of the strip, press again. Repeat with the other strip.

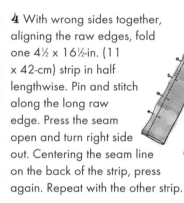

5 Insert the short sides of the handles between the outer fabric and the lining, positioning the ends ¾ in. (2 cm) from the side seams. Pin and slipstitch all around. For extra strength, topstitch all around the opening if you wish.

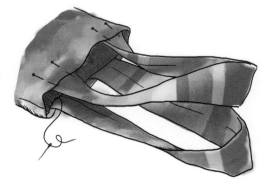

tricolore pillow cover

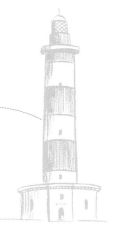

Coastal style can be very elegant: I believe it's just a matter of picking the right colors and keeping the design simple. In this project, the colors are, of course, reminiscent of the French flag. Flipping the front and back, so that the stripes are the other way around, is an easy way of giving the piece a more sophisticated and graphic quality. Hop onboard and make your own...

You will need

Two 21¼ x 11¼-in. (53 x 28-cm) rectangles of striped fabric

Two 21¼ x 5-in. (53 x 13-cm) rectangles of navy blue cotton fabric

Two 21¼ x 3½-in. (53 x 8-cm) rectangles of red cotton fabric

Two 21¼ x 5-in. (53 x 13-cm) rectangles of white cotton fabric

20 x 20-in. (50 x 50-cm) pillow form (cushion pad)

Sewing machine

Basic sewing kit (see page 129)

Matching sewing threads

Finished size: 20 x 20 in. 50 x 50 cm)

Skill level:

Sewing time: 1½ hours

Take ⅝-in. (1.5-cm) seam allowances unless otherwise stated.

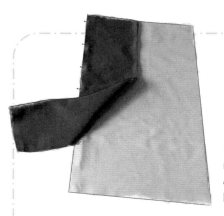

1 With right sides together, pin and machine stitch one striped rectangle and one blue rectangle together along one long side.

2 With right sides together, aligning the raw edges, pin and machine stitch the red strip to the navy blue side of the panel from step 1.

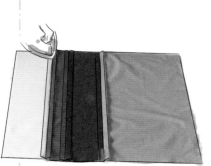

3 With right sides together, aligning the raw edges, pin and machine stitch the white strip to the red side of the panel. Press all the seams open. The back of the cover is now complete.

4 Repeat steps 1–3 to make the front of the cover.

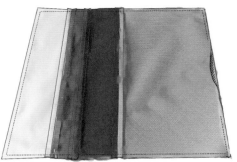

5 Place the front of the cover right side up on your work surface, with the striped edge on the left-hand side. Place the back on top, right sides together, with the striped edge on the right-hand side. Pin and machine stitch all around, leaving an 11-in. (28-cm) opening in the center of one side. Trim the seam allowances and snip off the corners. Turn the cover right side out.

6 Slip a 20 x 20-in. (50 x 50-cm) pillow form (cushion pad) inside the cover and slipstitch the opening closed (see page 133).

fabric pinwheels

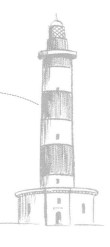

Pinwheels are fun and always bring a smile to my face! I remember I always asked my parents to buy one for me during our summer vacations in the windy Landes area of south-west France. Grab your favorite coastal prints and some interfacing and make this pinwheel decoration. It's a great alternative to a wreath for your front door—and, of course, it would be perfect for a beach cabin.

You will need

Heavyweight iron-on white interfacing

One 8-in. (20-cm) square of boat-wheel patterned fabric

One 8-in. (20-cm) square of anchor-patterned fabric

Two 2¾-in. (7-cm) squares of boat-wheel patterned fabric

One 2¾-in. (7 x 7-cm) square of anchor-patterned fabric

One 4-in. (10-cm) square of anchor-patterned fabric

Six self-cover buttons, approx. ⅝ in. (1.5 cm) in diameter

Scraps of fabric to cover buttons

60 in. (1.5 m) grosgrain (petersham) ribbon, 1 in. (2.5 cm) wide

Basic sewing kit (see page 129)

Matching sewing threads

Skill level: 🧵🧵

Sewing time: 2 hours

Take ⅝-in. (1.5-cm) seam allowances unless otherwise stated.

1 Following the manufacturer's instructions, apply interfacing to the wrong side of all the fabric squares.

2 Using an air-soluble fabric marker, working on the interfacing side, draw two lines diagonally across each square from corner to corner, intersecting in the middle. Make a pencil mark about one quarter of the way from the center in each direction. Cut along the pencil lines, stopping at the mark.

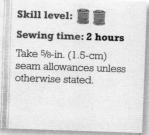

3 To form the pinwheels, bring every other point to the center of the square and secure temporarily with a pin. Repeat on all six squares of fabric.

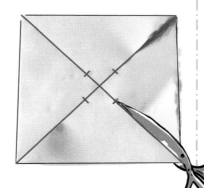

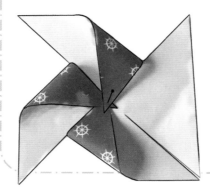

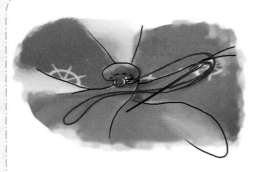

4 Following the manufacturer's instructions, cover six self-cover buttons with contrasting fabric. Sew one to the center of each pinwheel, securing the points in place.

5 With the right side facing up, place the two large pinwheels side by side on your work surface so that they lay intertwined. Using a thread and needle, secure them together using a few small stitches.

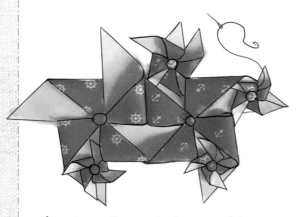

6 Put the smaller pinwheels on top of the large ones and secure them with small stitches.

7 Place the pinwheels on your work surface, right side down. Fold the grosgrain ribbon in two and place it on top, with the folded end of the ribbon sticking out by about 2¾ in. (7 cm) at the top. Using white thread and a needle, hand stitch the ribbon to the pinwheels with small stitches. Cut the ribbon ends in a V-shape.

Tip Because you are stitching on a three-dimensional piece with many loops, chances are that the stitches securing the ribbon to the pinwheels will look very irregular from the wrong side: it won't show, so don't worry about this!

Méhari frame

The Méhari is a vintage French car that was sold during the 1970s and 1980s. Cheap and light, this off-roader was mostly used for leisure activities. Many can still be spotted even today on the French coasts. Frame this classic appliqué silhouette and hang it in your hallway to welcome your guests!

You will need

Frame

Strips of gold natural silk

5 x 7 in. (12 x 18 cm) red cotton fabric for the appliqué

Gold satin ribbon, ¼ in. (7 mm) wide

Template on page 139

5 x 7 in. (12 x 18 cm) fusible bonding web

Sewing machine

Basic sewing kit (see page 129)

Craft knife and self-healing cutting mat

Pen

Double-sided tape

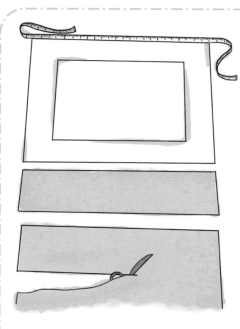

Skill level:

Sewing time: 1 hour

Take ⅝-in. (1.5-cm) seam allowances unless otherwise stated.

1 Take the back off the frame and remove the window mat (mount). Measure the long side of the window mat and cut strips of gold silk fabric to this length and about 2 in. (5 cm) wide; cut as many as you need to fit the height of the mat.

2 With right sides together, aligning the long raw edges, pin and machine stitch the strips together. Don't worry about stitching perfectly straight for once— you want to achieve a natural, rough look. Press the seams open. Depending on the weight of the fabric, you may need to trim the seam allowances.

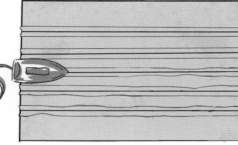

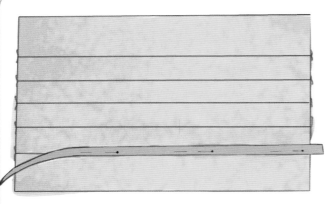

3 Working on the right side of your fabric panel, place a ribbon over the bottom seam line. Pin it in place, then topstitch along the center of the ribbon.

4 Trace the template on page 139 onto the paper side of the fusible bonding web. Following the manufacturer's instructions, iron the bonding web onto the back of the red cotton fabric. Using a sharp craft knife on a self-healing cutting mat, cut out the car silhouette.

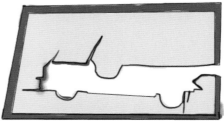

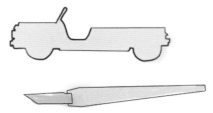

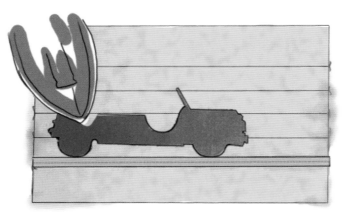

5 Peel the backing paper off the bonding web, place the fabric silhouette on the fabric panel with the wheels touching the top edge of the satin ribbon, and press in place.

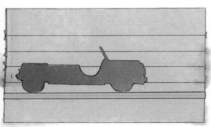

6 Write *Bienvenue!* ("welcome!") on the bottom right corner of the window mat (mount). Cut the appliqué to about 1 in. (2.5 cm) bigger all around than the aperture, then use double-sided tape to stick it in place. Reassemble the frame.

Tip How about replacing the Méhari silhouette with a 2CV— probably the most famous of all French vintage cars?

beach towel

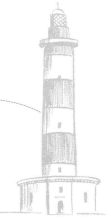

Whether you are aiming for the smart style of the Bordeaux area or the glamor of Saint-Tropez, this beach towel, with its classy burgundy and navy-blue ribbon stripes, will set you apart in style. Make one for each family member, using the same materials to achieve a cohesive ensemble but varying the weaving of the ribbon strips to personalize each one.

Skill level: 🪡

Sewing time: 1½ hours

Take ⅝-in. (1.5-cm) seam allowances unless otherwise stated.

You will need

125 in. (312 cm) navy blue grosgrain (petersham) ribbon, about 1 in. (2.5 cm) wide

122 in. (310 cm) burgundy grosgrain (petersham) ribbon about 1 in. (2.5 cm) wide

32 in. (80 cm) toweling, 60 in. (150 cm) wide

Sewing machine

Basic sewing kit (see page 129)

Matching sewing threads

1 Cut the burgundy ribbon in half. Then cut the navy blue ribbon into two 32-in. (80 cm) lengths and one 61-in. (152-cm) length.

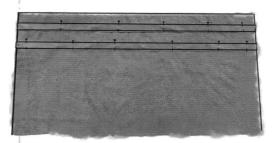

2 Place the toweling right side up on your work surface. Pin one short length of blue ribbon along one short edge, 1½ in. (4 cm) from the edge. Pin the second short length of blue ribbon 1½ in. (4 cm) from the first.

3 Pin the 61-in. (152-cm) blue ribbon strip along the left-hand side of the toweling, 1½ in. (4 cm) from the raw edge, weaving it under the first blue ribbon and over the second. Turn under each end of the ribbon to align with the toweling's selvages (selvedges). Topstitch along the long sides of all three ribbon strips, using blue for the top thread and burgundy for the bobbin thread.

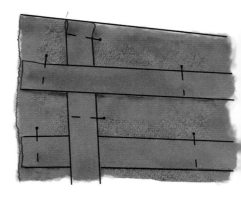

Tip This project takes advantage of the toweling's finished selvages (selvedges) to reduce the amount of sewing required.

5 Fold the burgundy ribbons over to the wrong side of the toweling and pin in place. Slipstitch in place along both edges.

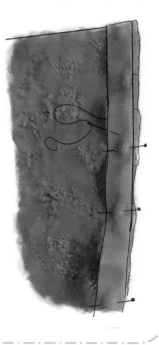

Pin one length of burgundy ribbon along each long ⌐w edge of the toweling, folding the ends under so that ⌐ey are level with the selvages (selvedges). Machine ⌐ch ⅜ in. (1 cm) from the edge.

Breton top

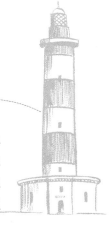

The Breton top is a classic piece in French fashion. Many French people own one, probably because some famous designers have made this piece much more than just a traditional sailor's garment: think Chanel and Jean Paul Gaultier! This top will give a little French touch to a child's wardrobe: it will look sweet on both boys and girls.

You will need

Pattern pieces G, H, I from pull-out pattern sheet

40 in. (100 cm) striped knit fabric, 55–60 in. (140–150 cm) wide

Scrap of red cotton fabric

Sewing machine

Basic sewing kit (see page 129)

Matching sewing threads

Skill level:

Sewing time: 3 hours

Take $5/8$-in. (1.5-cm) seam allowances unless otherwise stated.

1 Place tracing paper on top of the pattern sheet and trace off pattern pieces G, H, and I, in your chosen size (S, M, or L). Cut out the pieces.

2 With right sides together, fold the fabric in three, bringing the selvages (selvedges) together at the center. Pin the pattern pieces onto the fabric, following the layout guide. Note that front and back pieces are cut on the fold. Transfer the sleeve cap center mark onto the sleeve pieces. All seam allowances are included, so all you need to do is to trace the pattern pieces onto the fabric with a water-soluble pen or tailor's chalk and cut the fabric along those marks.

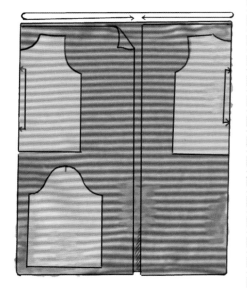

3 Zigzag stitch or serge (overlock) all raw edges.

4 With right sides together, aligning the raw edges, pin the front to the back along the shoulders. Machine stitch, then press the seams open.

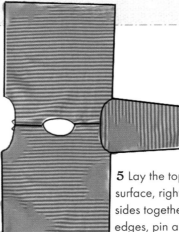

5 Lay the top flat on your work surface, right side up. With right sides together, aligning the raw edges, pin and stitch the first sleeve to the top. The mark at the top of the sleeve cap should align with the shoulder seam. The sleeves have a front and back: make sure you are using the correct sleeve, checking your pattern pieces if necessary. Repeat with the second sleeve on the opposite side. If necessary, especially with thicker fabrics, trim the seam allowances.

6 Fold the top back to its normal shape, wrong side out. Pin the underarm seams and the sides and stitch together. Trim and clip the seam allowances if necessary. Turn right side out.

Tip When sewing with knit fabric, use a stretch needle and select a stretch stitch if your machine has it; otherwise use a medium zigzag stitch.

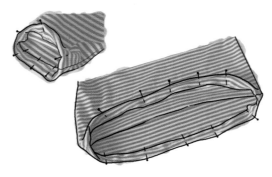

7 To hem the base of the top and the cuffs, fold over ⅝ in. (1.5 cm) to the wrong side, pin, and stitch close to the fold, using a twin stretch needle if you have one.

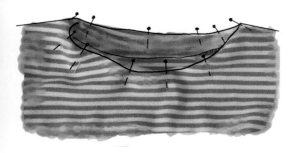

8 Hem the neckline by folding ⅜ in. (1 cm) over to the wrong side. Pin and stitch close to the fold. Again, use a twin stretch needle if you have one.

9 Cut a 3½ x 1¾-in. (8.5 x 4.5-cm) rectangle of red fabric. Fold it in two lengthwise with right sides together. Machine stitch along the short sides and the long raw edge, taking a ⅜-in. (1-cm) seam allowance and leaving a 1¼-in. (3-cm) opening in the middle of the long side. Trim the seam allowance and clip the corners. Turn right side out and topstitch along both long sides.

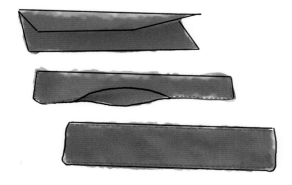

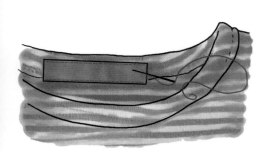

10 Using thread and a needle, hand stitch the label's short sides to the wrong side of the back of the neckline, making small stitches that go through the seam allowance only.

CHAPTER 5

Paris, je t'aime

Paris: city of lights and, of course, city of love! Get a feel of the city with these projects, both chic and sweet.

make-up pouch

Nothing could say "France" more than this zipped make-up pouch, with its cute blue, white, and red Eiffel Tower print! Did you know that the Eiffel Tower, built for the 1889 World's fair, was only meant to stay up 20 years? Luckily it's still there and has become an iconic symbol of the city. This very Parisian-looking pouch is just the right size for your face powder, lipstick, and eyeliner and even offers inside pockets to help you get organized.

You will need

Four 9½ x 2-in. (24 x 5-cm) rectangles of polka-dot print fabric

Two 9½ x 4-in. (24 x 10-cm) rectangles of Eiffel Tower print fabric

Four 9½ x 2-in. (24 x 5-cm) rectangles of Eiffel Tower print fabric

Two 9½ x 4-in. (24 x 10-cm) rectangles of polka-dot print fabric

One 2 x 4-in. (5 x 10-cm) rectangle of polka-dot print fabric

One 9½ x 6-in. (24 x15-cm) rectangle of polka-dot print fabric

6 in. (15 cm) narrow red velvet ribbon

One 9-in. (23-cm) closed-end zipper

Matching sewing threads

Sewing machine

Basic sewing kit (see page 129)

1 With right sides together, pin and machine stitch one 9½ x 2-in. (24 x 5-cm) polka-dot strip to each long side of one 9½ x4-in. (24 x 10-cm) Eiffel Tower piece. Press the seams open. Repeat to make another identical outer panel.

2 With right sides together, pin and machine stitch one 9½ x 2-in. (24 x 5-cm) Eiffel Tower strip to each long side of a 9½ x 4-in. (24 x 10-cm) polka-dot piece. Press the seams open. Repeat to make another identical lining panel.

3 Fold the 2 x 4-in. (5 x 10-cm) polka-dot strip in half lengthwise, wrong sides together, and press. Open out. Along both long sides, fold over ⅜ in. (1 cm) to the wrong side and press. Fold along the center crease line again and stitch along one long side close to the folds.

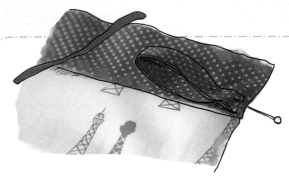

4 Fold the strip in two widthwise. Aligning the raw edges, place it on the right-hand side of one of the outer panels, at the base of the top polka-dot section. Pin and machine baste ⅜ in. (1 cm) from the edge. Hand stitch the ribbon to that same outer panel wherever seems fit, depending on the print. Make a bow.

5 Along one long edge of the 9½ x 6-in. (24 x 15-cm) polka-dot rectangle, fold ¾ in. (2 cm) over to the wrong side and press. Repeat and pin. Machine stitch close to the fold.

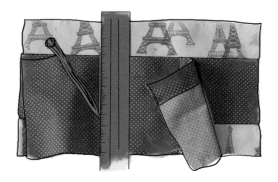

6 Place one lining panel right side up on your work surface. Pin the panel made in step 5 on top, also right side up, aligning the bottom and side edges. Using tailor's chalk or a water-soluble fabric marker pen, draw two vertical lines down the top panel, dividing it into thirds. Machine stitch along the lines, stitching through both layers.

7 Place the panel from step 6 pocket side up on your work surface. Lay the zipper along the top edge of the fabric, with the zipper pull facing up. Place one outer panel right side down on top. Pin all three layers together and, using a zipper foot, stitch along the top edge.

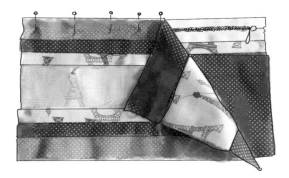

8 Fold back the outer and lining panels so that the wrong sides are together. Press gently.

9 Place the remaining lining piece right side up on your work surface. Place the zipped panel right side up on top. Finally, place the remaining outer piece on top, right side down, aligning the top edges. Pin all three layers together and, using a zipper foot, stitch along the top edge.

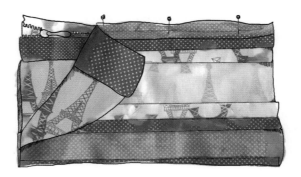

10 Open the zipper halfway. Bring both sides of the lining to one side, right sides together, and both sides of the outer panel to the other side, right sides together. Pin and machine stitch all around, taking a ⅜-in. (1-cm) seam allowance and leaving a 3-in. (7-5-cm) opening on the bottom edge of the lining panels. Snip off the corner and turn right side out.

11 Slipstitch the opening closed, then tuck the lining back in.

Tip If your fabric has a directional print (as in the Eiffel Tower print used for this project), be sure to place your panels in the right direction when assembling them.

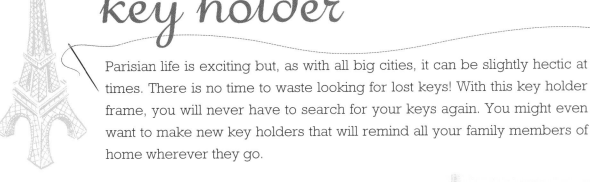

key holder

Parisian life is exciting but, as with all big cities, it can be slightly hectic at times. There is no time to waste looking for lost keys! With this key holder frame, you will never have to search for your keys again. You might even want to make new key holders that will remind all your family members of home wherever they go.

You will need

Frame with pre-cut mat (mount)

Scraps of four different fabrics

Iron-on interfacing (optional)

Four small hooks

Four keyrings

10 in. (28 cm) grosgrain (petersham) ribbon

Sewing machine

Basic sewing kit (see page 129)

Matching sewing threads

Hand drill and bit

Spray glue

Skill level:

Sewing time: 1 hour

Take ⅝-in. (1.5-cm) seam allowances unless otherwise stated.

1 Measure the width of your mat (mount) aperture. Divide by four and add 1¼ in. (3 cm); this gives you the width of the strips of fabric to be framed. Measure the height of the frame and add 1¼ in. (3 cm); this gives you the length of the strips. Cut four strips in four different fabrics.

   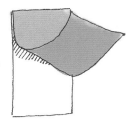

2 If necessary, apply interfacing to any lightweight strips, following the manufacturer's instructions: the four strips need to be of a similar stiffness.

3 With right sides together, aligning the raw edges, pin and stitch two strips together along one long side. Attach the third and fourth strips in the same way. Press the seams open.

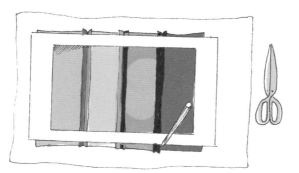

4 Place the fabric panel wrong side up on your work surface. Lay the mat (mount) on top, making sure that it is centered over the strips, and trace all around. Cut away any excess fabric and frame the panel.

5 Make four marks on the bottom of the frame, level with the center of the fabric strips. Drill a hole at each marked point and insert a hook into each hole.

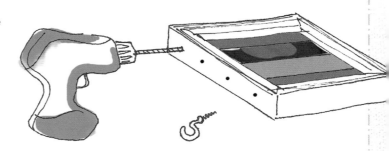

6 To make each individual key holder, measure one framed strip and cut two additional strips to that size in the same fabric. Apply interfacing if necessary to stiffen the fabric. Cut the grosgrain (petersham) ribbon into four equal lengths. Fold each ribbon in two and loop it through a keyring. Place one strip of fabric on your work surface, wrong side up. Place the ribbon ends on the strip, apply spray glue to the surface, and place the second strip right side up on top, aligning the raw edges. Press firmly. Using a hand stitch or machine zigzag stitch, stitch all around.

café apron

Cafés are a big part of French culture. In Paris, many people still have a quick espresso at the counter before they even start the day and go about their way. Most cafés serve croissants, while some of the most authentic places offer boiled eggs as a quick and nourishing snack. The waiters, traditionally called *garçons de café* (coffee-house "boys"), wear long aprons, from the waist down. The pockets at the front are especially convenient for a notepad, pencil, bottle opener, and change.

You will need

One 43 x 34-in. (110 x 85-cm) rectangle of white mediumweight cotton fabric

Two 2½ x 34-in. (6 x 85-cm) rectangles of white mediumweight cotton fabric

Two 1½ x 24 in. (4 x 61-cm) rectangles of white mediumweight cotton fabric

Matching sewing threads

Sewing machine

Basic sewing kit (see page 129)

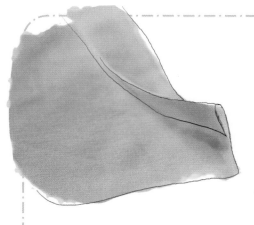

Skill level: 🏺🏺

Sewing time: 1½ hours

Take ⅝-in. (1.5-cm) seam allowances unless otherwise stated.

1 On one long side of the 43 x 34-in. (110 x 85-cm) panel, fold over ⅝ in. (1.5 cm) to the wrong side and press. Then fold over 1¼ in. (3 cm), press, pin, and machine stitch close to the fold.

2 Place the fabric panel right side up on your work surface. Working on side that you hemmed in the previous step, fold over 8 in. (20 cm) and press. Fold over 3½ in. (9 cm) in the opposite direction, press and pin in place. These pins will remain in place until step 6.

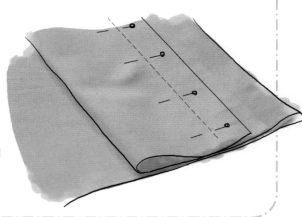

3 To make the ties, use the 2½ x 34-in. (6 x 85-cm) strips. On the first strip, fold one short edge over to the wrong side by ⅝ in. (1.5 cm). Fold the strip in two lengthwise, with wrong sides together, and press. Open the fold. Bring the long raw edges to the center crease and then fold the strip in two lengthwise again. Pin and stitch. Repeat with the other strip.

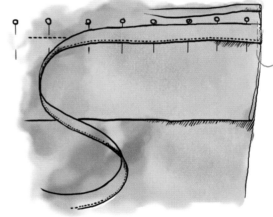

4 Place the apron right side up on your work surface. Place one of the ties on top with the raw end aligned with one side of the apron and the stitch line of the tie aligned with the stitch line made in step 1. Baste (tack) in place. Repeat on the opposite side of the apron, using the second tie.

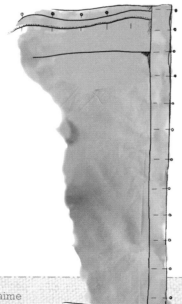

5 Fold one short edge of a 1½ x 24-in. (4 x 61-cm) strip over to the wrong side by ⅝ in. (1.5 cm). With right sides together and the folded over end aligned with the top of the apron, pin the strip down one side of the apron. Machine stitch ⅜ in. (1 cm) from the edge. Repeat on the opposite side, using the other strip.

6 Fold the side strip over to the wrong side of the apron. Fold under ⅜ in. (1 cm) of the strip to the wrong side and press. Pin and stitch close to the fold. Repeat on the opposite side. You may now remove the pins from step 2.

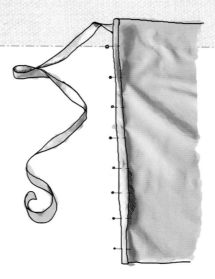

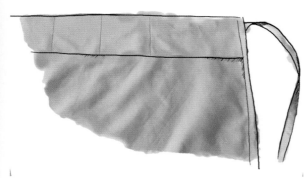

7 To make the front pockets, measure 8 in. (20 cm) in from one side of the apron. Using tailor's chalk or a water-soluble fabric marker, mark a vertical line across the folds that lie at the top of the apron. Mark two more vertical lines, 4 in. (10 cm) apart, and machine stitch. Repeat on the other side of the apron, stitching a total of six vertical lines.

8 Hem the apron by folding over ⅜ in. (1 cm) twice to the wrong side. Pin and stitch all layers.

Tip Little kitchen helpers will want their own apron. Simply reduce the length and width of the main panel and the side strips, and the length of the ties.

A-line skirt

The A-line skirt is both casual and chic: I believe you can never be overdressed or look scruffy while wearing one! It has clean, simple lines and looks great on most figures. For a classic French look, go for any solid color. Alternatively, give it a contemporary twist by selecting some graphic patterned fabric; my advice is to choose one with small, repeating motifs.

You will need

Pattern pieces J, K, L, M from the pull-out pattern sheet

3⅓ yards (1.2 m) of patterned fabric 44–45-in. (110–115-cm) wide

Iron-on interfacing (optional)

About 40-in. (1 m) of bias tape

8-in. (20-cm) closed-end zipper

Hook-and-eye closure

Sewing machine

Basic sewing kit (see page 129)

Matching sewing threads

> **Tip** Select a mediumweight cotton for this pattern. You can even use quilting cotton: its stiff quality suits this silhouette well.

Skill level: ▮▮▮

Sewing time: 3½ hours

Take ⅝-in. (1.5-cm) seam allowances unless otherwise stated.

1 Place tracing paper on top of the pattern sheet and trace off pattern pieces J, K, L, and M in your chosen size (XS, S, M, L, or XL). Cut out the pieces.

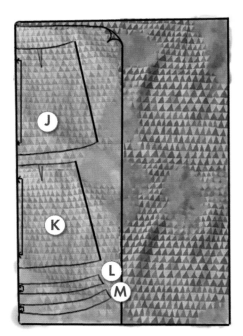

(J) Back
(K) Front
(L) Front hem facing
(M) Back hem facing

2 With right sides together, fold the fabric once, bringing the left-hand selvage (selvedge) to the center. Pin the pattern pieces onto the fabric, following the layout guide. Note that all pieces are cut on the fold. Transfer the zipper and dart marks onto the front and back pieces. All seam allowances are included, so all you need to do is to trace the pattern pieces onto the fabric with a water-soluble pen or tailor's chalk and cut the fabric along those marks.

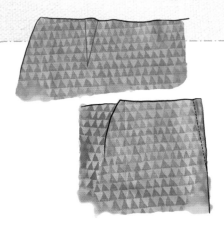

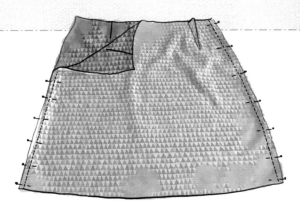

3 Fold the front fabric piece right sides together in order to align the dart marks. Pin and sew on the line, starting at the raw edges. Do not make backstitches at the point, but simply tie a knot with the thread tail. Repeat for the darts on the back piece.

4 Identify the left-hand side of the skirt front: placing the front piece on yourself might help. With right sides together, aligning the raw edges, pin and stitch the sides of the skirt, starting from the bottom and working your way up. Stitch all the way up on the right-hand side of the skirt; on the left-hand side of the skirt, stop at the zipper mark. Press the seams open. Turn the skirt right side out.

5 For extra stiffness, apply fusible interfacing to both hem facing pieces following the manufacturer's instructions; this is optional.

6 Place the front and back hem facings right sides together, pin, and machine stitch the short ends. Press the seams open.

7 With right sides together, aligning the raw edges, pin the hem facings around the skirt, making sure that side seams are aligned. Machine stitch the facings in place, then turn the skirt wrong side out.

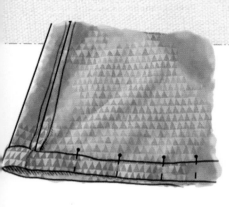

8 Fold the hem facings to the wrong side of the skirt and press. Fold under ⅜ in. (1 cm) along the top edge of the facings. Pin and stitch through all layers close to the fold.

9 Machine baste the seam allowance at the top of the left-hand side of the skirt. Press the seam open. Working on the wrong side of the skirt, place the zipper right side down, centering the teeth of the zipper along the seam, and hand baste in place. Using a zipper foot, stitch the zipper in place, then remove all the basting stitches.

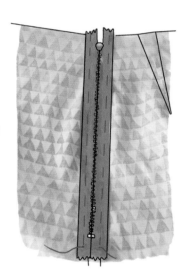

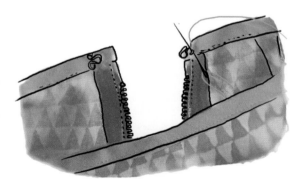

10 Bind the top of the skirt with bias tape (see page 135). Stitch a hook-and-eye closure above the zipper.

white cotton shirt

Many would agree that Parisian style could be defined as effortless chic. Staple wardrobe pieces include a little black dress, well-cut jeans, flats, a Breton long-sleeved top and ... a crisp, white shirt! This shirt is comfortable, but offers a clean-cut silhouette. It's made in seersucker, a fabric that's great for spring and summer. Simply add a little make-up and the legendary French confidence!

You will need

Pattern pieces N, O, P, Q from pull-out pattern sheet

35 in. (90 cm) seersucker fabric, 55–60 in. (140–150 cm) wide

30 in. (76.5 cm) bias-cut fabric, about 1 in. (2.5 cm) wide

5 x 3-in. (12.5 x 7.5-cm) rectangle of fabric matching the bias-cut fabric

5¼ x 4-in. (13 x 10-cm) rectangle of seersucker

One self-cover shank button, about ⅜ in. (1 cm) in diameter

Scrap of seersucker to cover the button

Sewing machine

Basic sewing kit (see page 129)

Matching sewing threads

Skill level:

Sewing time: 2½ hours

Take ⅝-in. (1.5-cm) seam allowances unless otherwise stated.

1 Place tracing paper on top of the pattern sheet and trace off pattern pieces N, O, P, and Q, in your chosen size (S, M, or L). Cut out the pieces.

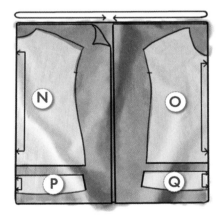
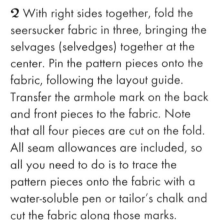

(N) Back
(O) Front
(P) Front hem facing
(Q) Back hem facing

2 With right sides together, fold the seersucker fabric in three, bringing the selvages (selvedges) together at the center. Pin the pattern pieces onto the fabric, following the layout guide. Transfer the armhole mark on the back and front pieces to the fabric. Note that all four pieces are cut on the fold. All seam allowances are included, so all you need to do is to trace the pattern pieces onto the fabric with a water-soluble pen or tailor's chalk and cut the fabric along those marks.

3 Zigzag stitch or serge (overlock) the shoulder and side edges to prevent the fabric from fraying.

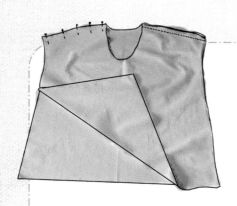

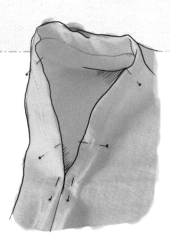

4 With right sides together, aligning the raw edges, pin the front to the back along the shoulders. Machine stitch, then press the seams open.

5 With right sides together, aligning the raw edges, pin the front and back together along the sides. Stitch from the bottom of the shirt to the armhole mark on each side, backstitching carefully at this point. Press the seams open.

6 Around the armholes, fold over ⅝ in. (1.5 cm) to the wrong side and press. Stitch within the seam allowances, pivoting twice per armhole.

7 Fold the 5 x 3-in. (12.5 x 7.5-cm) rectangle of fabric matching the bias in two widthwise. Pin, then machine stitch the sides. Trim seam allowances, turn right side out, and press. Repeat with the 5⅛ x 4-in.(13 x 10-cm) rectangle of seersucker.

8 Center the printed piece on top of the seersucker piece, aligning the raw edges. Machine baste along the raw edges, taking a ⅜-in. (1-cm) seam allowance.

9 Place the back hem facing on your work surface, right side up. Center the two small seersucker and printed fabric rectangles on the left-hand short side, aligning the raw edges. Place the front hem facing on top, right sides together. Pin the short sides of the facings together and machine stitch, stitching through all layers. Trim the seam allowances and press the seams open.

10 Fold the seersucker and printed fabric rectangles over so that they lie against the back hem facing. Cover the button with seersucker fabric and stitch it in place, stitching through all layers.

11 With the wrong side of the shirt facing the right side of the facing, aligning the side seams, pin the hem facing to the shirt. Machine stitch all around, taking a ⅜-in. (1-cm) seam allowance. Press the seam open and turn the facing to the right side of the shirt. Press again.

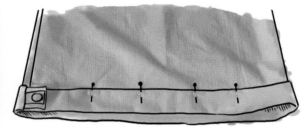

12 Along the raw top edge of the facing, fold under ⅜ in. (1 cm) to the wrong side. Pin and topstitch close to the fold.

13 Bind the neckline with the bias-cut fabric (see page 135), using the invisible bias binding technique.

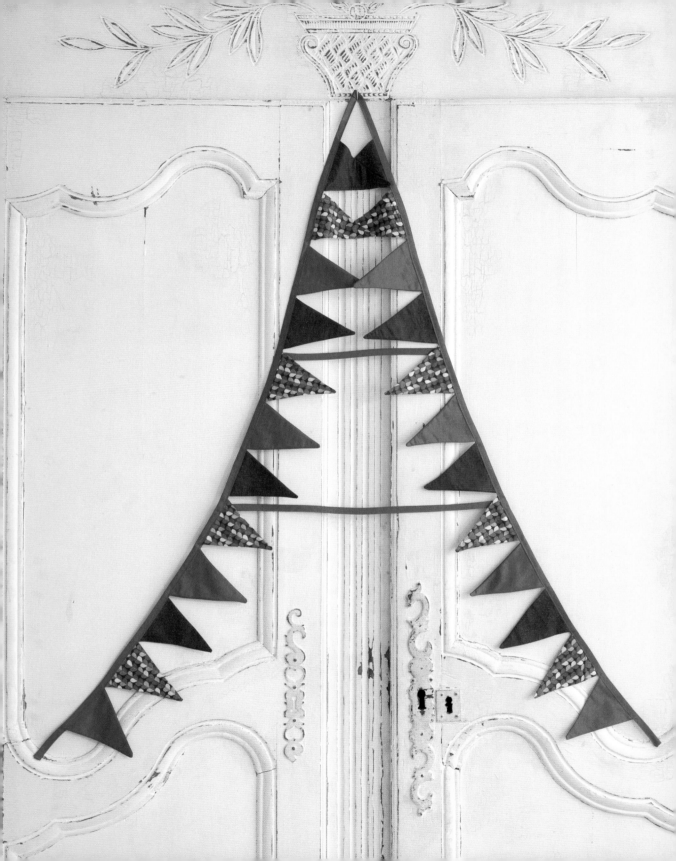

Eiffel banner

Shaped in what the French call *la vieille dame* ("the old lady"), this vertical banner is at once cheerful and a little eccentric—and since Paris is known the world over as the City of Love, it's a great opportunity to use some heart-patterned fabric. You could use this Eiffel Tower banner for a kid's room or as a decoration for a French-themed party or a surprise candlelight dinner.

You will need

Template on page 140

12 in. (30 cm) of red cotton fabric, at least 44–45 in. (110–115-cm) wide

12 in. (30 cm) of purple cotton fabric, at least 44–45 in. (110–115-cm) wide

12 in. (30 cm) of heart-patterned cotton fabric, at least 44–45 in. (110–115-cm) wide

3½ yards (3.2 m) single-fold bias tape

Sewing machine

Basic sewing kit (see page 129)

Matching sewing threads

Skill level:

Sewing time: 2½ hours

Take ⅝-in. (1.5-cm) seam allowances unless otherwise stated.

1 Using the template on page 140, cut 16 triangles from each fabric.

2 On the wrong side of eight of the red triangles, draw a ⅜-in. (1-cm) seam allowance along the two long sides. Repeat with eight of the heart-patterned and purple triangles.

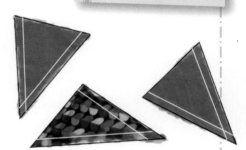

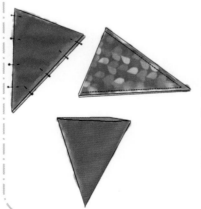

3 With right sides together, aligning the raw edges, pin the marked red triangles together in pairs with the unmarked triangles along the two long sides. Stitch along the marked lines, pivoting at the point. Trim the seam allowances and clip the corners. Turn right side out and press. Repeat with the heart-patterned and purple triangles.

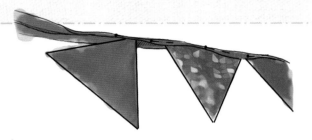

4 Fold over ½ in. (1 cm) to the wrong side at one short end of the bias tape and press.

5 Starting 2 in. (5 cm) from one end, start inserting the raw ends of the triangles into the bias tape, alternating red, purple, and heart-patterned triangles and placing them right next to one another. Pin as you move along. After the twelfth triangle, leave a 6¼-in. (16-cm) gap, and then start inserting triangles again, reversing the sequence of colors. After inserting the last triangle, measure 2½ in. (6 cm) and cut the bias tape. At the end of the tape, fold over ½ in. (1 cm) to the wrong side and press.

6 In the center of the gap between the two sets of triangles, fold the bias tape at a 50° angle, so that the triangles point inward. Stitch along the bias tape, securing the triangles in place and pivoting at the angle.

7 The two pairs of triangles at the top of the banner overlap: topstitch them in place along the long side that overlaps, from one side of the bias tape to the other.

8 Hang the banner to check that it is symmetrical. Counting from the top, measure the distance between the fourth pair of triangles (from one side of the bias to the other). Cut a strip of bias of tape to that length. Measure the distance between the fifth pair of triangles (bias to bias), counting from the bottom. Cut a bias strip of that length.

9 Pin the two strips of bias across the banner to mimic the floors of the tower, then hand stitch them in place.

lap tray cushion

Taking a few notes, writing a postcard, or even having a morning croissant and a cup of black coffee: you can do all this and more with this comfortable lap tray cushion. I've made this project in urban green and feminized it with an edging of seagreen polka dots—ideal for the mellow atmosphere of a Parisian boudoir.

You will need

Thin wooden board or plywood

Water-based paint

Two 10-in. (25-cm) strips of self-adhesive hook-and-loop tape, ¾ in. (2 cm wide)

Mediumweight green fabric (see box on page 125)

Lightweight polka-dot fabric (see box on page 125)

Polyester toy filling

Paintbrush

Basic sewing kit (see page 129)

Tape measure and scissors

Matching sewing threads

Extra-strong glue

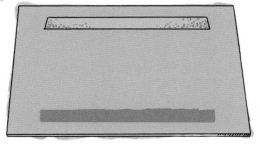

1 On one side of the board, draw a 10 x ¾-in. (25 x 2-cm) rectangle, ¾ in. (2 cm) in from each long side. Paint the board on both sides, except these two rectangles. Pull the two strips of hook-and-loop tape apart and glue the hook side of each strip onto an unpainted rectangle.

2 Place the wooden board on the wrong side of the green fabric and draw around it twice, using tailor's chalk or a water-soluble pencil. Cut out the rectangles of fabric ⅝ in. (1.5 cm) beyond the chalk or pencil lines.

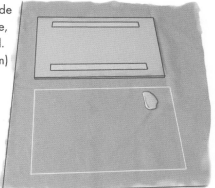

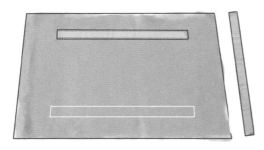

3 On the right side of one of the green panels, draw a 10 x ¾-in. (25 x 2-cm) rectangle, ¾ in. (2 cm) in from each long side of the chalked rectangle. Place the loop sides of the hook-and-loop strips in these rectangles and topstitch them in place.

4 Cut four strips of polka-dot fabric 2½ in. (6 cm) wide x the width of the green panels. Fold ⅜ in. (1 cm) over to the wrong side along one long edge of each strip. Place one green rectangle on your work surface, right side up. Place a polka-dot piece right side up along each short side, aligning the raw edges. Topstitch along the inner edge of each polka-dot strip, close to the folds. Repeat with the other green rectangle panel.

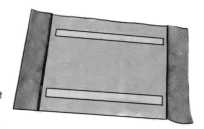

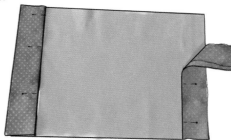

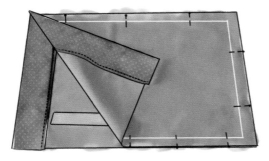

5 Place both panels right sides together. Pin and machine stitch all around, stitching along the chalk line that you drew in step 2 and leaving an opening on one short side. Turn right side out.

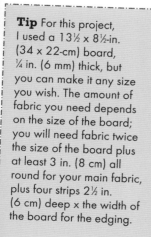

6 Fill the cushion with stuffing and slipstitch the opening closed (see page 133). Attach the cushion to the wooden board via the hook-and-loop tape.

garment cover

Paris is a capital of *haute couture*, with famous designers, extravagant collections, and long catwalks. Behind the scenes, there's a little less glamor, a lot of highly skilled workers, and a lot of patient handstitching! To protect your special garments, a zipped garment cover is an accessory that you cannot do without. You could even embroider some running stitches to pay tribute to the skill and patience of generations of unknown garment makers.

You will need

White cotton fabric, at least 45 in. (115 cm) wide (see box)

Piping in a contrasting color (see box)

One 22-in. (55-cm) closed-end zipper

Matching sewing threads

Embroidery floss (thread) to match piping and needle

Pattern pieces R, S, T from pull-out pattern sheet

Tracing paper, paper for pattern, and pencil

Sewing machine

Basic sewing kit (see page 129)

1 Place tracing paper on top of the pattern sheet and trace off pattern pieces R, S, and T. You will need one of each piece. Measuring from the top center of the template pieces, add whatever length is needed to fit the garment (see box). Pin the pattern pieces to the wrong side of the fabric: note that the back piece R is cut on the fold. Draw around the pattern pieces with a water-soluble fabric marker pen or tailor's chalk and cut the fabric along those marks.

2 Prepare the piping, following the instructions on page 136.

3 From what is left of the white cotton, cut a strip measuring 2 in. (5 cm) x the length of piece S. With right sides together, aligning the raw edges, pin then machine stitch the piping to one long side of the strip.

Skill level: 🧵

Sewing time: 2 hours

Take ⅝-in. (1.5-cm) seam allowances unless otherwise stated.

How much fabric? Measure the length of the garment for which you are making the cover. Add 7 in. (18 cm). This gives you the length of fabric and piping you will need. It could be anywhere between 1 and 2 yards (90 and 180 cm), depending on the garment. It is also the total length of the template pieces.

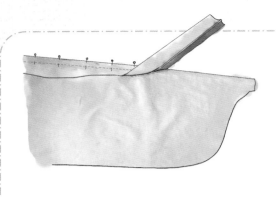

4 With right sides together, aligning the raw edge of the piping and the long side of piece S, pin and stitch the pieces together. Press the strip open so it becomes the new edge of the panel.

5 Following the instructions on page 138, insert the zipper between panels S and T, positioning the top of the zipper 8 in. (20 cm) from the top of the fabric panels.

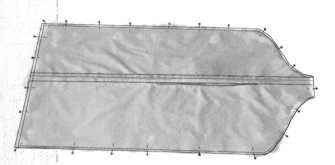

6 Place back piece R right side up on your work surface. Open the zipper halfway and place the zipped panel right side down on top, aligning the raw edges. Pin and stitch all around, leaving the short, straight top edge open. Trim the seam allowances and snip off the corners. Turn right side out and press.

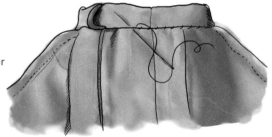

7 At the top of the garment cover, turn ⅜ in. (1 cm) over to the wrong side and press. Repeat , then slipstitch.

8 Using embroidery floss (thread) and an embroidery needle, work a line of running stitches ⅜ in. (1 cm) long following the bottom and side seams.

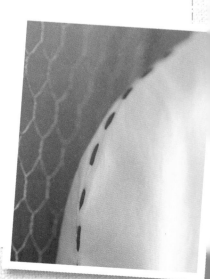

tools & techniques

Basic sewing kit

Apart from a sewing machine, you will need a basic sewing kit. For pinning, cutting, marking, tracing, and measuring, this is what you need to get started.

Pins Small, regular pins are fine for most projects. The thick ones come in handy for heavyweight fabrics and batting (wadding). Don't forget to remove pins as you stitch and to throw away any twisted ones.

Scissors It doesn't really matter if your scissors are designed specifically for sewing or not, as long as their blades are sharp and clean. Note that you should not use this pair for anything else; keep a separate pair for cutting out paper patterns and templates. Pinking shears come in handy and will occasionally save time, but are not an absolute necessity to get started.

Tape measure More convenient than a ruler when dealing with fabric, tape measures are usually 60 in. (150 cm) long.

Tracing tools You will often need to trace on fabric, usually on the wrong side, and occasionally on the right side (for topstitching purposes). Use white tailor's chalk for dark colors and any color for light-colored fabrics. An air-erasable or water-soluble pencil for fabric is great, too. If you own neither of those tools, you can use a bar of soap (simply cut sharp edges with a knife). You will also need tracing paper for patterns and templates and a long ruler. I like metallic rulers, as they weigh more on the tracing paper and the fabric, which helps to keep everything in place.

Set of needles This is necessary to close openings or to finish details by hand. Use thinner needles for the lighterweight fabrics and thicker ones for multiple layers and thick fabrics.

Matching threads Most of the time, using the same quality for the upper and bobbin threads will prevent problems with thread tension and save some precious time.

You will also need An iron and ironing board are essential: keep them close by, as you will need to iron seams and panels often. A comfortable chair at your sewing table is important to prevent back pain, as is a higher table or working surface so that you can work standing up when tracing patterns or laying out and cutting large panels of fabric.

Using patterns and templates

Several projects in this book require that you use patterns and templates. Here is how to do it.

Garment patterns Pattern pieces for the garments in this book are presented in several sizes. Select the size you usually dress in when buying garments from a store.

Fabric has to be folded in two or three, bringing the selvages (selvedges) to the center or aligning one on the other. Always fold fabric right sides together so that you can trace on the wrong side of the fabric. All pattern pieces include seam allowances (specified in each project): you do not add any to the pattern pieces.

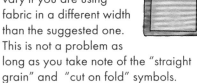

A layout guide is included for each garment, helping you to position the pattern pieces on the fabric. Note that the layout of the pattern pieces will vary if you are using fabric in a different width than the suggested one. This is not a problem as long as you take note of the "straight grain" and "cut on fold" symbols.

Straight grain The straight grain of the fabric, parallel to the selvages (selvedges), is indicated by a double-headed arrow.

Cut on fold If you need to align a pattern piece with one of the folded edges of the fabric, thus forming perfectly symmetrical pieces, this symbol is used.

Templates Most templates can be traced using tracing paper. Simply place tracing paper over the template, draw over the shape, and cut out with scissors. Place the template on the wrong side of the fabric, pin it in place, and draw around it with tailor's chalk or a water-soluble pencil. Remove the pins and template and cut out the fabric. All templates include seam allowances (indicated for each project) where required. You do not need to add any.

Stitching seams

There are various ways of stitching seams; these are the basic ones used in this book.

Basic seam

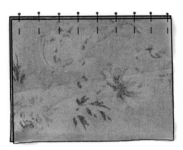

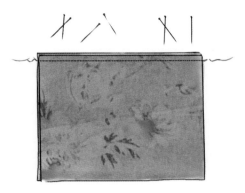

1 Place two pieces of fabric right sides together, aligning the raw edges. Usually, pins are placed at a right angle to the seam line, pointing toward the inside of the fabric panel. At times, pins will be positioned along the seam.

2 Set your machine to a regular straight stitch, then lower the foot and the needle. Before you start stitching, make sure you are using the correct seam allowance. At the beginning and end of each seam, unless otherwise stated, make a few backstitches.

Machine basting Occasionally you will need to machine baste: just set your machine to a long stitch and do not work any backstitches at the beginning and end of stitching.

Turning corners When you reach a corner, stop stitching ⅝ in. (1.5 cm)—or whatever seam allowance you are using—from the edge of the fabric. Using the balance wheel, lower the needle into the fabric. Then raise the presser foot and pivot the fabric around until your needle is aligned with the next seam line.

Treating seam allowances

You will often need to trim or cut into seam allowances, either to get rid of excess fabric and prevent bulkiness or for ease in curves, corners, or crossed seams. On straight seams, trim the seam allowances to about ¼ in. (5 mm) after stitching. Always press seams open unless otherwise stated.

Curves On curved seams, cutting into the seam allowance will make it easier for the fabric to lie flat. On both inward and outward curves, stop cutting about ⅛ in. (3 mm) from the stitching and press the seam allowance open.

Corners On right-angle corners, trim away the tip of the seam allowance. Then taper the side seam allowances toward the point. Press the seams open on both sides.

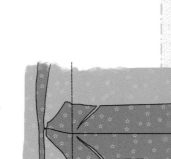

Inward curves For inward curves, clip wedge-shaped notches out of the seam allowance at regular intervals.

Crossed seams When stitching together pieces that already have seams, you may create some bulk and tension on the seams. Press the first seam open and stitch the second seam. Snip off the points of the first seam. If you feel there may still be some tension on the seams, make a couple of slits within the seam allowances pointing outward, and press open.

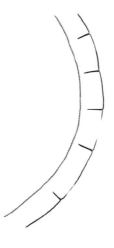

Outward curves For outward curves, simple slits are enough. The deeper the curve, the closer together the slits should be.

Slipstitch

This stitch is very useful for closing an opening that you left to turn a project right side out. It's an easy stitch that is used throughout this book.

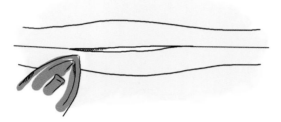

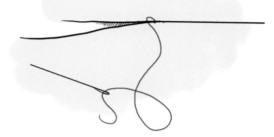

1 First, mark a crease that will guide your stitching. With your project wrong side out, press the seams allowances open, including the opening.

2 Thread a needle and knot the end of the thread. Where the stitching is interrupted, slip the needle from the underside and draw it up through the crease. The knot is invisible, lying within your project.

3 Slip the needle through the fold on the opposite crease and bring it back up about ⅜ in. (1 cm) farther along on the same side. Then slip the needle into the opposite crease again. Repeat until you reach the end of the opening.

Bias binding

Bias is the line going diagonally across the grain of the fabric. It is slightly stretchy and therefore a good option to mold around curves such armholes and necklines—as a substitute facing, for example.

Making bias binding Bias tape is, by extension, a strip of fabric cut on the bias. You can buy pre-cut bias tape in most fabric or notions stores, but you may need to make your own if you can't find the perfect color or want your bias to match your fabric perfectly.

1 Fold the fabric diagonally to form a 45° angle. Press and unfold.

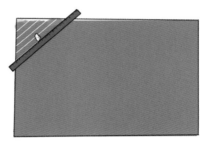

2 Using the crease as reference, draw parallel lines 1½–2 in. (4–5 cm) wide across the fabric, using tailor's chalk or a water-soluble pencil. Cut the strips along the drawn lines.

Joining strips of bias binding You may need to join strips together to make the length of bias tape you need.

1 First, square off the ends of the strips being joined. Then pin the ends of the strips at 90° to each other, with right sides together.

2 Stitch across the right-angle corner and cut off the excess fabric.

3 Fold the top strip up along the stitching line, so that it is right side up, then turn the whole strip over and press the seam allowance open.

Attaching bias tape When attaching bias tape, you have two options: sewing the bias tape so that it is visible on the outside of your project (as in the skirt on page 112) or, for a more discreet look, sewing the bias tape so that it is invisible from the outside (as in the shirt on page 116). Before you attach the bias strip to the project, fold it in two lengthwise and press lightly. Open up the bias strip again. Bring one long raw edge to the center crease and press. Bring the opposite long edge to the center, along the first. Your bias strip is now ready for use.

Visible bias binding

1 Open up the bias tape. With the wrong side of the fabric against the right side of the bias tape, aligning the raw edges, pin the bias tape along the edge of the piece being bound. Machine stitch along the first crease line.

2 Trim 1/16 in. (2 mm) from the seam allowances. Press the seam allowances toward the bias tape.

3 Fold the bias tape over to the right side of the fabric, then fold the bias tape under along the crease line, so that it barely covers your first stitch line. Pin in place.

4 Machine stitch along the edge of the bias tape, close to the folded-under edge.

Invisible bias binding

   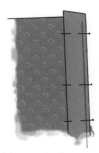

1 With right sides together, aligning the raw edges, pin the bias tape along the edge of the piece being bound. Machine stitch along the first crease line.

2 Working on the wrong side, press the seam allowances toward the bias tape.

3 Stitch within the seam allowance as close to the seam line as you can (understitching).

4 Fold over the bias tape to the wrong side. Fold under the fabric along the nearest crease line, pin in place, and machine stitch close to the fold.

Making piping

To make piping, you will need bias-cut strips and piping cord. The width of the strips you need to cut depends on the width of your seam allowances and the width of your cord. Double the width of your cord and double the width of your seam allowance. Add those two measures and you get the width of the bias strips you need to cut.

1 Place a bias-cut strip on your work surface, wrong side up. Place the cord in the middle and fold over the fabric over the cord, aligning the raw edges. Pin.

2 Attach a zipper foot to your machine and set your machine to a long stitch. Stitch along the fabric, as close to the cord as possible.

Attaching piping Attaching piping is not difficult but it requires a little patience in order to achieve satisfying results—especially when dealing with curves.

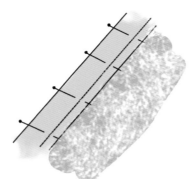

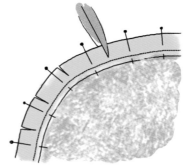

1 With right sides together and aligning the raw edges, pin the piping along the edges of the fabric panel, with the pin points facing in toward the center of the fabric. Using a regular stitch and a zipper foot, stitch along the piping, as close to the cord as possible.

2 To manage curves with ease, before you attach the piping snip the seam allowance of the piping as close to the stitches as you can without cutting through them. Using a regular stitch and a zipper foot, stitch along the piping, as close to the cord as possible.

Mitering corners
When sewing for the home, you will very often need to finish or hem a right-angle piece. Here is how to do it with ease.

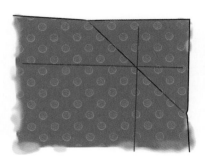 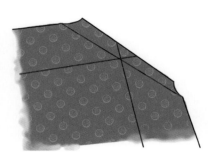 

1 Using tailor's chalk or a water-soluble pencil, draw lines along each side of the fabric 2 in. (5 cm) in from the raw edges. At the point where the lines intersect, fold the corner in toward the center, forming a right-angle triangle. Press well to mark the diagonal crease. Reopen.

2 Draw a line parallel to the crease, ³⁄₁₆ in. (5 mm) out from the crease. Cut off the corner along this mark. Fold the fabric back toward the center along the crease line.

3 Fold the raw side edges in along the lines you drew in step 1.

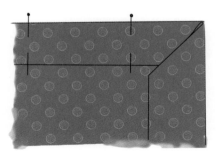 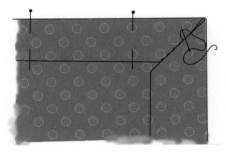

4 Fold the raw edges under by ³⁄₁₆ in. (5 mm). Pin and stitch close to the fold, pivoting at the corner.

5 For lightweight fabrics, work a few slipstitches along the miter.

Inserting a centered zipper

Don't shy away from the projects that need a zipper. Follow these detailed steps and remember that careful preparation (pressing and basting/tacking) is the key to success.

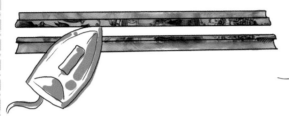

1 Prepare the panels that are to be zipped together. Along one edge of one panel, turn over ⅝ in. (1.5 cm) to the wrong side and press. Repeat with the other panel. Open out the folds.

2 With right sides together, aligning the raw edges, pin one panel to the other. Stitch along the crease, leaving an opening the length of the zipper in the middle. Using contrasting thread and setting your machine to a long stitch, pin and stitch along the fold line over the opening. Do not make backstitches, as these stitches will be removed later. Press the seam open.

3 Place the panel on your work surface, wrong side up. Pin the zipper on top, right side down, centering the teeth of the zipper on the seam line. Again using contrasting thread, secure with hand basting (tacking) stitches.

4 Turn the panel right side up. If necessary, open the zipper halfway so that you will be able to turn the piece right side out. Stitch the zipper in place along the zipper tape. There is no need to keep the stitches close to the teeth so you don't need to use a zipper foot. Once you are done, remove all the basting (tacking) stitches.

templates

The templates on pages 139–140 are shown at 100%, so you can simply trace them off the page, while the templates on page 141 are shown at 50%, so you'll need to photocopy them at 200% to print them at the correct size.

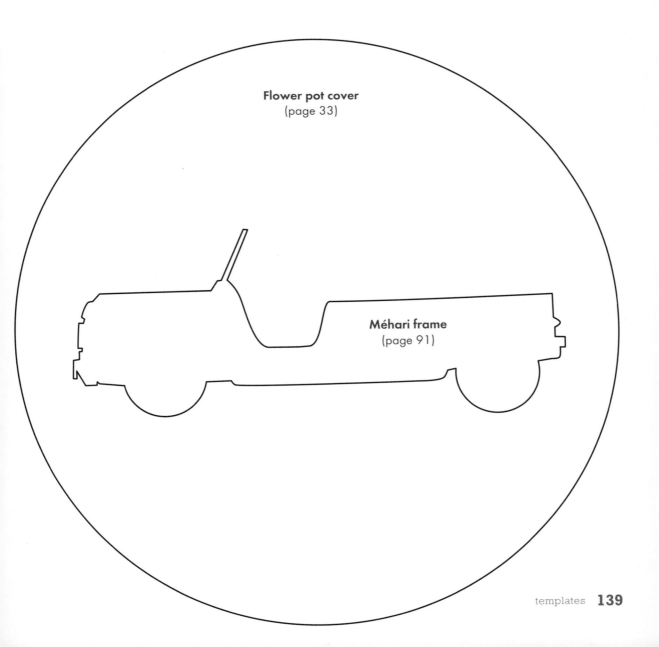

Flower pot cover
(page 33)

Méhari frame
(page 91)

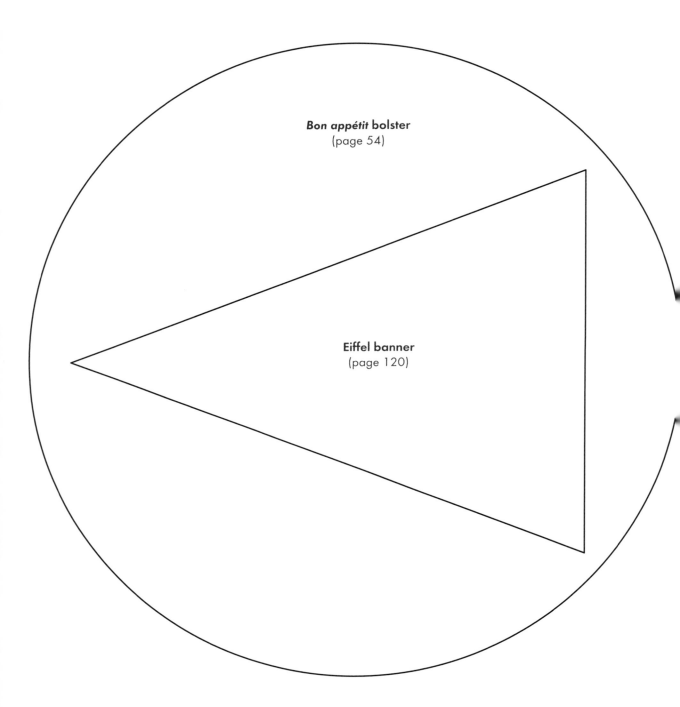

Bon appétit bolster
(page 54)

Eiffel banner
(page 120)

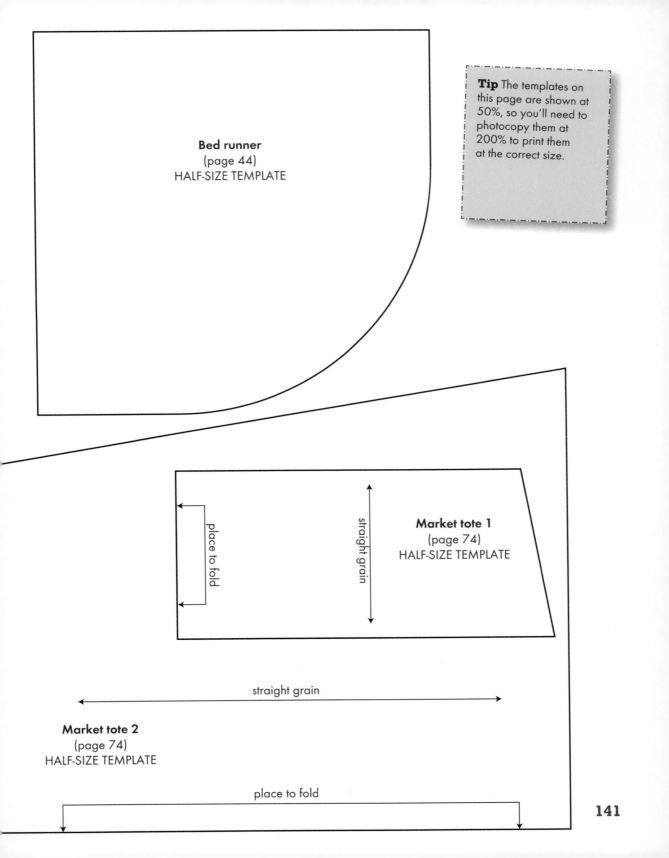

Bed runner
(page 44)
HALF-SIZE TEMPLATE

Tip The templates on this page are shown at 50%, so you'll need to photocopy them at 200% to print them at the correct size.

place to fold

straight grain

Market tote 1
(page 74)
HALF-SIZE TEMPLATE

straight grain

Market tote 2
(page 74)
HALF-SIZE TEMPLATE

place to fold

suppliers

French suppliers

Artiga
Artiga specializes in Basque stripes. They have several stores, mostly in the southwest of France, and you can also buy online.
www.artiga.fr

Pierre Frey
A high-end and very French-looking online home furnishings store.
www.pierrefrey.com

Les Olivades
A very nice fabric brand, including a range of Provençal-style fabrics.
www.lesolivades.fr

Tissage de Luz
Tissage de Luz specializes in Basque fabrics. They have two stores in the southwest of France and you can also buy online.
www.tissagedeluz.com

Tissus Reine
3–5 Place St Pierre
75018 Paris
www.tissus-reine.com

Vêtement Marin Broderie
Lots of good-quality Breton stripes fabrics, perfect for marinières. Online sales only.
www.vetement-marin-broderie.com

US suppliers

A. C. Moore
www.acmoore.com

Amy Butler Design
218 Mt Parnassus Drive
Granville, OH 43023
Tel: +1 740-587-2841
www.amybutlerdesign.com

Fabric Depot
700 SE 122nd Avenue
Portland, OR 97233
Tel: +1 503-252-9530
www.fabricdepot.com

Fabricland
855 US-22 West
North Plainfield, NJ 07060
Tel: +1 908-755-4700
www.fabricland.com

Jo-Ann Fabric and Craft Stores
5381 Darrow Road
Hudson, OH 44236
Tel: +1 888-739-4120
www.joann.com

Michaels
Tel: 1-800-642-4235
www.michaels.com

Mood Fabrics
225 West 37th Street,
3rd Floor
New York, NY 10018
Tel: +1 212-730-5003
www.moodfabrics.com

Purl Soho
459 Broome Street
New York, NY 10013
Tel: +1 212-420-8796
www.purlsoho.com

Vogue Fabrics
718–732 Main Street
Evanston, IL 60202
Tel: +1 847-864-9600
www.voguefabricsstore.com

UK suppliers

Kleins
5 Noel Street
London W1F 8GD
Tel: +44(0) 20 7437 6162
www.kleins.co.uk

John Lewis
300 Oxford Street
London W1A 1EX
Tel: +44(0) 20 7629 7711
www.johnlewis.com

Liberty
Regent Street
London W1B 5AH
Tel: +44(0) 20 7734 1234
www.liberty.co.uk

MacCulloch & Wallis
25–26 Dering Street
London W1S 1AT
Tel: +44(0) 20 7629 0311
www.macculloch-wallis.co.uk

Ray Stitch
99 Essex Road
London N1 2SJ
Tel: +44(0) 20 7704 1060
www.raystitch.co.uk

VV Rouleaux
102 Marylebone Lane
London W1U 2QD
Tel: +44(0) 20 7224 5179
www.vvrouleaux.com

Truro Fabrics
Lemon Quay
Truro
Cornwall TR1 2LW
Tel: +44(0) 1872 222130
www.trurofabrics.com

index

size conversion chart

The adult patterns on the pull-out sheet are given in sizes small, medium, and large, except the A-line skirt, which also includes extra small and extra large. The conversions are below:

	France	US	UK	Europe
XS	36	6	8	34
S	38	8	10	36
M	40	10	12	38
L	42	12	14	40
XL	44	14	16	42

The child's Breton top sizes are for ages 4–5 years old, 6–7 years old, and 8–9 years old.

acknowledgments

I would like to thank CICO for giving me the opportunity to do this book. I would also like to thank everyone who worked on this book, especially Sarah Hoggett for editing the book with such care and expertise and Carmel Edmonds for her kind assistance throughout the process, making this an incredibly exciting and smooth experience from start to finish.

Thank you to Caroline Arber for the pretty photography, Nel Haynes and Catherine Woram for the great styling, Harriet de Winton for the delicate step illustration, Tom Forge for the beautiful design, Stephen Dew for the precise pattern illustration, and Michael Hill for the French "icon" illustrations. The French feel of the book owes a lot to all of you. Merci à tous!